The Ring by Spring Ruse is a compassionate and faith-filled guide for single women who feel discouraged by waiting and weary of cultural pressure. With honesty, humor, and biblical wisdom, Grace McCready exposes the lies many of us unknowingly believe about dating and replaces them with hopeful truths rooted in God's Word. This book is a timely encouragement, reminding readers that waiting isn't wasted and that God's plans are always worth trusting.

— Courtney J. Burg,
author of *Loyal to a Fault: How to Establish New Patterns When Loving Others Has Left You Hurting*

The Ring by Spring Ruse is a generous breath of fresh air for every woman experiencing discouragement in dating and wondering about God's plan for her future. Grace McCready's relatable experiences provide good company along this sometimes confusing and often emotional journey. She brilliantly counters ten false narratives with real-life examples that bring clarity, perspective, and fun. Thank you, Grace, for this gift of hope!

— Susie Crosby,
author of *Lighthearted 100-Day Devotional: One Word Promises to Lighten Your Load and Lift Up Your Heart*

The Ring by Spring Ruse

Recognizing and Rewriting the False Narratives Single Girls Have Been Told About Dating and Waiting

Grace McCready

All names have been changed to protect the privacy of the individuals. Exceptions are as follows: the sisters of the author, the single girls and former single girls who shared their stories for this book, and the individuals mentioned by the single girls and former single girls who shared their stories for this book.

Cover design by Hannah Linder Designs

ISBN 979-8-218-89682-9 (pbk.)

ISBN 979-8-218-89683-6 (eBook)

"Wait for the LORD; be strong and let your heart take courage; yes, wait for the LORD."

Psalm 27:14 (NASB)

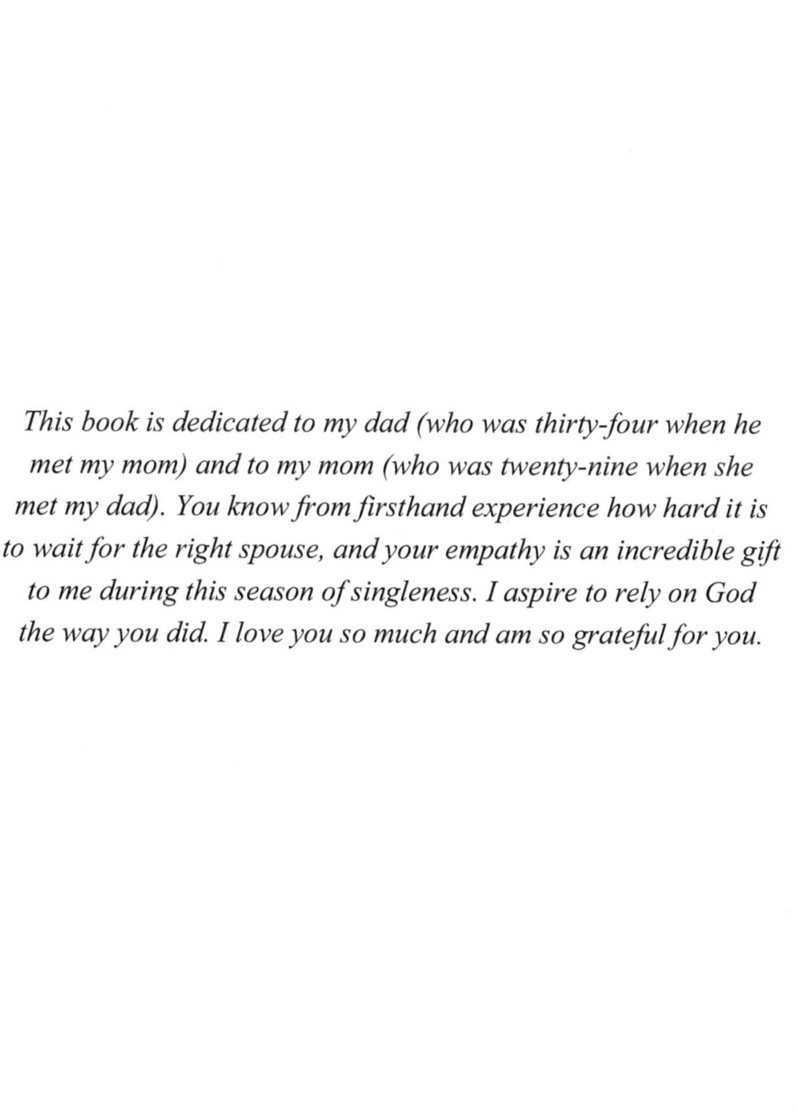

This book is dedicated to my dad (who was thirty-four when he met my mom) and to my mom (who was twenty-nine when she met my dad). You know from firsthand experience how hard it is to wait for the right spouse, and your empathy is an incredible gift to me during this season of singleness. I aspire to rely on God the way you did. I love you so much and am so grateful for you.

Contents

Chapter 1

Getting a Ring by Spring ~~Is~~ Isn't a Guarantee

Dear Single Girl,

I have a confession—actually, a few confessions—that I need to make. I've never had a boyfriend, a fiancé, or a husband. I've never held anyone's hand or kissed anyone. I've never received a love letter, a box of chocolates, or a bouquet of flowers from my significant other. I've never been told, "I love you" or "I want to spend the rest of my life with you."

I thought these experiences would've happened by now, but they haven't—and I've definitely had trouble accepting that at times. After all, I was under the impression that Christian girls get engaged by the time they graduate from college, especially if they attend Christian colleges. I thought getting a ring by spring was practically a guarantee.

When I finished high school, I did attend a Christian college. Even though my motive for choosing that specific school wasn't to find my future husband, I was still hopeful I'd get a ring by spring—or at least meet a guy who would one day buy me an engagement ring and marry me. While I was there, I made myself available by getting involved with on-campus and off-campus activities, plugging into a local church, and spending time with a variety of people. I didn't nervously run away from the boys on campus or lock myself in my dorm room for all hours of the day. I basically did everything I could possibly do to connect with guys, especially during my junior and senior years. But on my graduation day, I didn't have a ring, a boyfriend, or even a prospect.

"Getting a ring by spring is a guarantee" is one of the many false narratives I've heard about dating and waiting over the years. While these false narratives typically contain *elements* of truth, they aren't *fully* true. Unfortunately, because they're often laced with truth, it can feel practically impossible to expose and refute them. To be honest, I've believed several false narratives about dating and waiting, and I've struggled with disappointment as a result. I've even given in to despair.

But the Lord has helped me realize that as long as I wait on Him, I have no reason to despair. Even though I didn't expect my life to look like this, I know this is exactly how it's supposed to look. My lack of a ring by spring isn't a coincidence. In fact, it's one of the main reasons I wrote this book.

Single Girl, if you also lack a ring by spring and you opened this book because of that reality, you came to the right place. As a fellow single girl, I have lots of personal stories and scriptural truths to share with you. I'm here to offer you encouragement in this challenging season of life.

Although I don't know if or when you'll find love because I don't know God's plan for you, I know nothing can prevent His plan from coming to pass. If it's His will for you to find love, you'll find it because He'll provide it. In the meantime, we'll rewrite ten of the most prevalent and pervasive false narratives about dating and waiting so we can be strong and take courage while we trust Him together.

Love, Grace

//

Though I wasn't allowed to date until I was eighteen, I was pretty okay with that. Honestly, I didn't know many great guys. But I assumed that would change at college. I also assumed the exponential increase in the number of eligible bachelors in my life would lead to an exponential increase in the number of dates I got. (Spoiler alert: I was wrong.)

When I graduated from high school, I went to a Christian college that was hundreds of miles from home and in a culture that was very different from the one I grew up in. Less than a thousand students lived on campus, but I loved that the student body was so small. Having been homeschooled from kindergarten through twelfth grade, going to college there didn't feel as intimidating as going to college at a huge state university. It didn't take long for me to start recognizing names and faces.

From the baseball team (which was the largest group on campus since there weren't enough students for a football team) to the theater group (which was the smallest group on campus since there were approximately five people majoring in theater), the college provided a community for young people to live, learn, and grow together. During my time there, I had opportunities to tutor other students, teach piano lessons, lead a discipleship group, speak at a vespers service, and play keyboard in chapel. Though not all the students there were Christians, I was confident many of them were.

But when my graduation day arrived, I realized I hadn't been on a *single* date during my four years of college—and the guy I'd *wanted* to date *still* didn't know I was alive.

Let me share a quick backstory about him. His name was Sean, and I actually developed a crush on him when I was a junior in high school and he was a junior in college. My older sister was a freshman at the same college, and from the moment she showed me his picture in the online directory, my heart was set on him. A couple years later, I started attending that college too. I was a freshman with high hopes for us, and he was a senior without any such hopes.

It didn't take long for me notice Sean's best feature—his adorable smile. His mouth curved slightly to the side so I could barely see his teeth. Then again, maybe his best feature was his chocolate-colored hair that swept across his forehead (but not like Justin Bieber's hair in 2011). His tan complexion was also quite attractive. His skin never seemed to burn, unlike mine. I was attracted to his athletic build as well. He was the perfect amount of tall—not so tall that he looked like a giraffe but tall enough that he could tilt his head down to kiss me (not that I'd thought much about it, of course).

In addition to all those things, Sean was a Christian who appeared to live out his faith. He was kind, confident, handsome, smart, and athletic. He was a soccer player and a resident assistant with a great personality, and he was well-liked by basically everyone on campus. Plus, he was single. I never even saw him with a girlfriend. That made me very happy but also very curious.

Before I could figure out why Sean wasn't taken, he graduated. In fact, he graduated a semester *early*. That was a major bummer because I'd only had the chance to be on campus with him for a few months before he disappeared. I assumed I'd never see him again.

But fortunately, I did. He made a reappearance during my junior year of college. He took a job as the resident director of one of the guys' dorms, and I couldn't have been more thrilled.

This is our chance! I thought. *Now he'll definitely fall in love with me. We'll be married by the time I graduate.*

However, the college had a rule that staff members couldn't date students, so I quickly realized that Sean and me dating wasn't going to happen—at least not until I graduated. I thought that *maybe just maybe* he'd still fall in love with me somehow, even though we technically couldn't date. But he was nowhere close to even knowing I existed, let alone falling in love with me. In fact, during the five semesters when we both lived on campus at the same time, we interacted approximately twice.

Our first interaction happened during my freshman year. I was carrying way too many things in the cafeteria, and I accidentally dropped my fruit on the floor. As I inwardly groaned at my clumsiness, Sean came over to help me pick up my runaway grapes. I was pleasantly surprised. "Thank you" were the only words I could utter before he walked away. But I was confident wedding bells would be ringing in the not-too-distant future.

Our second interaction occurred when I was a senior. (Yup, three years had passed since Sean and I had had a conversation; the idea of us getting married might've been a little far-fetched.) I was sitting at a table where students could sign up to join discipleship groups because I'd decided to lead one that semester. As Sean was leaving the cafeteria, he stopped by the sign-up table to talk to the girl sitting next to me because he was planning to lead a discipleship group too. Honestly, I wasn't even part of that conversation—but I *felt* like I was. I hadn't been in such close proximity to Sean since the grape incident, and I was thrilled we were both going to be discipleship group leaders. I assured myself that we'd have great conversations together as a result. But no such conversations ever happened.

When I graduated from college, I couldn't help but hope that Sean and I would start dating since I was no longer a student (and thus he was permitted to date me). Instead, I found out he was engaged. A few months later, he got married.

Absolutely *nothing* came from the *six years* I spent daydreaming about Sean. I finished college with a diploma but no ring—and the guy from whom I wanted a ring gave it to someone else. I was confused and devastated.

Single Girl, God knows the very best way for you to meet your future husband. If you believe you won't find love beyond college, it might be time to refocus on who God is. He can do beautifully unexpected things in beautifully unexpected ways. Getting a ring by spring is certainly a possibility, but if it doesn't happen, you can trust He has a better plan.

//

Then Job replied to the LORD:

> "I know that you can do anything,
>
> and no one can stop you.

You asked, 'Who is this that questions my wisdom with such ignorance?'
It is I—and I was talking about things I knew nothing about,
things far too wonderful for me.
You said, 'Listen and I will speak!
I have some questions for you,
and you must answer them.'
I had only heard about you before,
but now I have seen you with my own eyes.
I take back everything I said,
and I sit in dust and ashes to show my repentance."
(Job 42:1-6 NLT)

After suffering countless losses—and questioning God's goodness and wisdom as a result—Job came to the right conclusion. He recognized his lack of understanding and humbly repented. God's purpose for his suffering was so much greater than he could comprehend, and he finally accepted that.

Like Job, we frequently think, speak, and act on things we know nothing about—things far too wonderful for us to ever understand. Based on our extremely limited knowledge, we make assumptions like these: "I'm going to meet my future husband when I'm a college freshman, get engaged when I'm a college senior, and get married when I graduate." When we assume we're in control of our destinies, it's natural to feel discouraged when we realize we're not. But God can transform our discouragement to hope as He shows us that He can do *anything* and that *nothing* can stop Him.

Even though I gradually began to accept that Sean and I weren't meant to be together, the acceptance process was still very hard. I remember returning to my college campus about six months after my graduation to attend a Christmas concert. I noticed Sean sitting a few rows ahead of me with his new wife, and I suddenly felt the urge to scream, "Sean could've been mine, God! Why isn't he mine?"

In that moment, I wasn't ready to hear God's answer—but He did answer. (And eventually, I listened.) He whispered, "Grace, I'm not keeping Sean *from* you; I'm keeping you *for* someone better."

More recently, I found a prayer I wrote at the beginning of my senior year of college: "Help Sean pursue me—but only if it's Your will. If it's not Your will, I'm okay with that. Please make room in my heart for whoever will be mine someday." During my senior year, God started to answer that prayer as I slowly recognized Sean wasn't meant for me—and He fully answered that prayer when Sean got married the following year. That's when I *knew* Sean wasn't meant for me. But in order for God to make room in my heart for my future husband, He had to take Sean out of it. So He did.

Single Girl, if your plan for getting a ring by spring didn't come to pass, don't despair. Though it might *feel* like your one and only chance to meet your future husband has come and gone, I *promise* God is still at work. Finding love isn't about high probabilities or favorable odds; it's about having faith in the One who does the impossible.

There's nothing wrong with making plans, but ultimately, you shouldn't put all your confidence in them because God alone is worthy of your full confidence. His plan for you—including His plan for how you'll meet your future husband—is perfect. And as Job learned, absolutely nothing can thwart His plan.

//

Alli's Story

Our twenties—especially our college years—tend to be a confusing time because we're figuring out who we are and what kind of people we want to be. But when we experience our twenties (or even a portion of them) as single women, we can really focus on what we want to do in life. We can create goals that don't involve other people, like boyfriends or husbands.

I was single throughout college, and my experience with singleness was full of ups and downs. One day, I'd feel free and empowered. The next day, I'd feel so lonely it physically hurt. However, my years of singleness were some of the best years of my life because I used that time to invest in myself and my relationship with God—and ultimately, to figure out who I was.

In my season of singleness, I felt so close to God because He was all I really had to focus on. One of my favorite things to do when I was single was go on "dates" by myself. While sitting in my favorite coffee shop, I wrote prayers in my journal. I went out for ice cream and even dinner alone. And during those "dates," I often thought about what kind of man would have to come along for me to be willing to give up my life as a single woman.

That kind of man did eventually come along—and I'm very happy he did. But now that I'm married, I can see singleness truly was a gift from God. I wouldn't trade that season for anything.

~Alli, Former Single Girl~

Chapter 2

Desiring Marriage ~~Is~~ Isn't Wrong

Dear Single Girl,

This might sound strange, but I shopped for wedding dresses online earlier this week. I don't know what came over me. I suddenly had the urge to see if the wedding dress I imagine myself wearing on my wedding day actually exists. (By the way, it does—but its affordability is a whole other story.) In addition to deciding what my dream wedding dress looks like, I've also determined my ideal hairstyle, playlist, and color scheme. The main thing I don't know about my wedding is whom my groom will be.

Who will be vowing to love, honor, and cherish me until death parts us? Who will be holding me close during our first dance as husband and wife? Who will be walking beside me as we leave the reception to spend our happily ever after together?

Sometimes, it feels like I'll never find out the answer to these questions. Sure, I can speculate about what my future husband will be like. But for now, he's simply a figment of my imagination.

Single Girl, if your curiosity about your future husband has morphed into fear, maybe you've given in to the temptation to pretend you don't really care about the whole marriage thing. Maybe you used to express interest in finding love, but because you haven't found it yet, you now feign disinterest in it. Maybe you've "sworn off guys," even though all you really want is a guy.

You don't have to pretend that being single is a dream come true for you. Frankly, I doubt that if I looked at your playlist, your streaming platform watchlists, and your bookshelf, I'd only see worship music, animal documentaries, and Bible commentaries. I'd probably see sappy love songs, beloved rom-coms, and new romance novels.

Yes, this season of singleness is where God wants you to be *now*, but that doesn't mean this is where He wants you to be *forever*. There's a balance between hating the waiting and acting like the waiting is your favorite place to be. Are you willing to admit to yourself—and others—that even though your husband isn't in your present, you're excited about the possibility of him being in your future?

Love, Grace

The first thing I ever wrote about singleness (and shared with the public) was a post for my blog. I entitled it "Are You Ready for a Romantic Relationship?" and published it in February 2018 in honor of Valentine's Day. In that post, I encouraged readers to ask themselves if they were ready to date—and I said *I* wasn't ready to date.

Hence the façade began. The façade of "I'm not ready yet." The façade of "There just aren't any mature guys in my life." The façade of "I'm content to pursue my personal aspirations rather than date and get married."

Frankly, I've desired a romantic relationship from the time I hit puberty, but singleness has haunted me ever since.

Perhaps one of the hardest parts of singleness is knowing God never promised I'd get married. Even though I feel like I have a husband-shaped hole in my heart, there are no promises in Scripture that He'll fill it. And that's a very difficult reality to accept.

I think most single girls struggle to accept that reality too. So they try to suppress their desire for marriage (and their connected desires for attention, affection, love, intimacy, and sex) as they gloss over the truth that God—who only creates good things—created the institution of marriage. But to be honest, they can't suppress their natural, God-given desires forever—at least, I couldn't.

During my senior year of college (when I had a slightly confused view of God's role in my life and His purpose for marriage), I wrote this prayer in my journal: "Show me You're able to satisfy my strong craving for a boyfriend."

There's nothing wrong with that prayer necessarily. It's essential to find my ultimate satisfaction in God. He alone is my Creator and Savior. No one else provides true peace or purpose.

However, in wanting my desire for a boyfriend to disappear, I neglected an important detail about marriage: God created marriage to complement—not take the place of—His relationship with men and women. Yes, they were made to know and love Him above everyone and everything, but they were also made to know and love each other. God's design included them joining together to become one flesh.

Over time, I came to understand that better. I realized my desire for a husband wasn't strange, sinful, or something I needed to "overcome." Rather, it was something God placed inside me when He made me.

Honestly, I believe that hidden underneath the façade of "I don't really want to get married" is the incredibly intense desire of well-meaning single girls who do indeed want to get married but simply haven't yet. I've seen this play out before. When a girl is single, she says she isn't really into the idea of getting married—until a guy asks her out on a date, which leads to a second date and a third date and a fourth date and (eventually) a marriage proposal. Then the wedding bells start ringing, and Miss I-Could-Take-It-or-Leave-It is gliding down the aisle in a white gown to pledge herself forever to a man she claimed she wasn't interested in even meeting.

Voilà.

I certainly don't blame any single girl for going out with a solid Christian guy, accepting his marriage proposal, or marrying him. I simply don't think it makes sense for a girl who's "perfectly content" being single to do that. If she's truly happy in her current season, she'll stay put. She'll remain single.

Inconsistencies like these are the main reason I wrote this chapter. I want single girls to know they'll feel freer in the long run when they understand and appreciate—rather than attempt to conceal or change—how God designed them. It's time for us to put away the pretense and honestly admit that even though we're not currently in romantic relationships, we do want to be.

While I was recovering from anorexia, my counselor told me I had to become comfortable with being uncomfortable. There were so many things going on inside me—physically, emotionally, mentally, and spiritually—that made me feel uncomfortable during recovery. I struggled to reconcile my feelings about my body with the objective truth about my body. Thankfully, my physical recovery didn't take very long, but it took several years for me to truly progress in my emotional, mental, and spiritual recovery. I finally began to make progress in those areas when I learned to become comfortable with being uncomfortable—to accept that not feeling okay is in fact okay.

Single Girl, becoming comfortable with being uncomfortable is exactly what you have to do too. I understand how difficult it is to be made for something you don't have yet—to reconcile your desire for a husband with the reality that he isn't here right now and might not be here for a while. But you don't have to fill this uncomfortable season of singleness with false claims like "I'm fasting from guys" or "I'm too busy falling in love with Jesus to date anyone" or "Chasing my dreams is more important to me than getting married." This season isn't about proving to yourself or others that you can thrive without a man in your life. The process of becoming comfortable with being uncomfortable starts with acknowledging and embracing the way God created you.

> Then the LORD God said, "It is not good for the man to be alone; I will make him a helper suitable for him." Out of the ground the LORD God formed every beast of the field and every bird of the sky, and brought them to the man to see what he would call them; and whatever the man called a living creature, that was its name. The man gave names to all the cattle, and to the birds of

> the sky, and to every beast of the field, but for Adam there was not found a helper suitable for him. So the LORD God caused a deep sleep to fall upon the man, and he slept; then He took one of his ribs and closed up the flesh at that place. The LORD God fashioned into a woman the rib which He had taken from the man, and brought her to the man. The man said,
>
> > "This is now bones of my bones,
> > And flesh of my flesh;
> > She shall be called Woman,
> > Because she was taken out of Man."
>
> For this reason a man shall leave his father and his mother, and be joined to his wife; and they shall become one flesh. And the man and his wife were both naked and were not ashamed. (Gen. 2:18-25 NASB)

I believe the number of women who are destined for lifelong singleness is very small, and I base this belief on Genesis 2:18-25. God created men and women, and He created them for marriage. This relationship isn't a result of the Fall; it's part of God's original design for humanity. He literally created Eve *from* Adam and *for* Adam—and for this reason, men should leave their parents, join with their wives in marriage, and become one flesh with them. When they follow God's design, they can experience unashamed intimacy.

I'm not suggesting that marriage is *superior* to singleness. (I'll talk more about my disdain for that false narrative in chapter 10.) *Both* seasons are valuable in God's sight. He graciously uses married people *and* single people to accomplish His work.

But unfortunately, the Church often groups all of our needs and desires into one category: the Jesus category. Yes, everyone ultimately needs a personal relationship with Jesus. There are no substitutes for that relationship.

Frankly, however, there are no substitutes for marriage either. Our need for salvation—for redemption through Christ alone—is very different than our desire for marriage—for the "one-flesh" relationship men and women were created for. God could've simply filled the void in Adam's life with more of Himself. Instead, however, He said it wasn't good for the man to be alone and created a wife for him—and she was exactly what he needed (Gen. 2:18-25).

Single Girl, being excited about marriage isn't bad. It's totally okay to look forward to what God has in store for the next season of your life as long as you're trusting and obeying Him in the current season too. Even in a world corrupted by the Fall, God's original design for men and women to join together in marriage remains.

Your desires for attention, affection, love, intimacy, and sex within marriage are normal and biblical. You don't need to be ashamed of your longing to be married or try to suppress it. In fact, I encourage you to acknowledge and embrace it. Even if having this unfulfilled longing is uncomfortable, you can have peace knowing the presence of this longing in your life isn't a sign that something is wrong with you; it's simply a sign that you're human.

Ally's Story

For me, singleness feels a little different because I was born and grew up with my person. My twin, Lexi, is worth more to me than all the words in the world. I believe God gave her to me to do life with, which I realize might sound a little confusing.

While I do desire a husband, I also fear Lexi will meet someone first and then leave me behind. I fear I'll lose the safe haven we've created together with her beautiful flowers, our sweet kitty, and the endless Hobby Lobby decorations covering every corner of our little apartment. I was chatting with Lexi about these fears last night, and she reminded me how crucial it is to be thankful for the *now*.

I think an important word that ties into this is contentment. I just finished a women's Bible study last week, and we used a book that gave examples of what contentment—and discontentment—can look like in different seasons of our lives. Books like that—in combination with much introspection and many conversations with Lexi—have led me to an eye-opening conclusion that I hope will help you as much as it's helped me: Be thankful for the *now* because you never know how short the *now* will be.

~Ally, Single Girl~

Chapter 3

Friendship ~~Is~~ Isn't Equivalent to Marriage

Dear Single Girl,

During my childhood, I had a close friend named Alexis. We were basically friends from infancy because we grew up at the same church. When we were older, we went to the same homeschool group too. She even came over to play when her older sister babysat me and my sisters.

Partway through seventh grade, however, Alexis moved away. Making new friends was *not* fun or easy. Although I had some in middle school and high school, I wasn't super close with them.

My first two years of college were similar. I started college full of expectation—and anxiety—about meeting new people. Over time, I developed a few friendships, but they weren't particularly deep. Then I met Avery during my junior year.

Single Girl, even though I had a huge crush on Sean at the time I met Avery, *he* didn't know I existed and *she* did. Avery noticed me when I desperately wanted to be noticed. And ultimately, I fell for the lie that friendship works as a substitute for marriage, which resulted in me getting hurt. I don't want you to get hurt too.

No matter how incredible a friendship is, it'll never be an equal substitute for marriage. As I mentioned in chapter 2, there are *no* equal substitutes for marriage. It uniquely reflects the relationship between Christ and the Church. Friendship, which doesn't involve a binding commitment between the two people involved, is a very poor substitute for something as sacred as that.

Love, Grace

//

I remember meeting Avery at the beginning of my junior year of college. When I first met her, I wasn't quite sure what to think about her. But my uncertainty didn't last long.

I was sitting by myself in the cafeteria one night when she walked over to my table and asked if she could sit with me. I said yes. So we started chatting over mediocre cafeteria food, and an hour later, she felt like my closest friend.

She asked such good questions, and she seemed like such a sweet person. Plus, we had several things in common. Our family structures and homeschool backgrounds were similar. Even though it was her first semester at the college, we were both juniors because she'd transferred from a different college. She wasn't dating anyone, and neither was I. It was so easy to talk with her and relate to her.

The next two years were filled with thoughtful compliments, intimate conversations, and long texts. It almost felt like we were dating. Don't misunderstand that though—our relationship wasn't romantic. We were both *solely* attracted to guys. But if Sean had said and done everything Avery said and did, I would've been head-over-heels in love.

Avery encouraged me to take care of my physical, emotional, mental, and spiritual health. She cared about my relationship with God, and she wanted to see me grow closer to Him. She said thoughtful things to me, bought kind gifts for me, and planned fun outings with me. No matter what we did together, I always had a great time with her.

The questions Avery asked me were deep and insightful. Frankly, though, her profound questions led me to share vulnerable—often *too* vulnerable—answers with her. I let down my guard with her *so* many times, but I pretended my unguardedness was acceptable because she was just my friend and I was just being transparent with her.

But I think that's when things started to go south with Avery—when I started treating her more like my husband than my friend. I had lengthy conversations with her, shared secrets with her, and told her I loved her. When we were together, she had my full attention. When we were apart, she was on my mind. Honestly, I was borderline obsessed with her.

Instead of saving my heart for my future husband, I carelessly gave it away to Avery. She didn't cherish it; she played with it. Eventually, she discarded it. Though I tried very hard to substitute my friendship with her for what I truly wanted, it didn't work.

Single Girl, I understand the temptation to try to substitute a relationship you *do* currently have for a relationship you *don't* currently have. But friendship and marriage aren't synonymous—and pretending they are will only lead to disappointment. Your heart is precious. Even if your friends are amazing, they don't deserve your heart. It'll only be truly safe in the care of the one who seeks to love you as deeply and faithfully as Christ loves the Church.

//

> Wives, be subject to your own husbands, as to the Lord. For the husband is the head of the wife, as Christ also is the head of the church, He Himself being the Savior of the body. But as the church is subject to Christ, so also the wives ought to be to their husbands in everything.
>
> Husbands, love your wives, just as Christ also loved the church and gave Himself up for her, so that He might sanctify her, having cleansed her by the washing of water with the word, that He might present to Himself the church in all her glory, having no spot or wrinkle or any such thing; but that she would be holy and blameless. So husbands ought also to love their own wives as their own bodies. He who loves his own wife loves himself; for no one ever hated his own flesh, but nourishes and cherishes it, just as Christ also does the church, because we are members of His body. FOR THIS REASON A MAN SHALL LEAVE HIS FATHER AND MOTHER AND SHALL BE JOINED TO HIS WIFE, AND THE TWO SHALL BECOME ONE FLESH. This mystery is great; but I am speaking with reference to Christ and the church. Nevertheless, each individual among you also is to love his own wife even as himself, and the wife must see to it that she respects her husband. (Eph. 5:22-33 NASB)

The concept of trying to substitute a non-romantic relationship for a romantic relationship might not sound super common or conventional initially, but single girls actually do it quite often. Feeling doubtful that their future husbands will ever enter their lives, some attempt to satisfy their desire for marriage with a different type of relationship—friendship. Unfortunately, this behavior is unintentionally encouraged by the Church at times. Being in community (which is a fancy phrase for fellowship) is discussed frequently, but guarding our hearts in the context of friendship isn't.

Is it important for us to have Christ-centered friendships built on transparency and trust? Definitely. But do our friends—who enter and exit our lives at various times—deserve full access to our hearts? Definitely not.

Friendship just isn't equivalent to marriage—at least not according to Scripture. Kelly Needham discussed this truth in her book *Friend-ish: Reclaiming Real Friendship in a Culture of Confusion*. I read *Friend-ish* to determine if my friendship with Avery was unhealthy, and honestly, the Holy Spirit used Kelly's words to convict me. In fact, it felt like Kelly was speaking directly to me when she described the distinctions between marriage and friendship:

> So is it okay for a friend to be more than a friend? Is it right for a friend to be your person? Let me answer with a clear *no*.
>
> The Bible is clear that marriage is the only relationship to be exclusive and binding. No other human relationship gets the title of "one flesh." No other human relationship has "you-belong-to-me" ownership. No other relationship calls for lifelong commitment (Gen. 2:24; 1 Cor. 7:4, 39). While there is one example of two friends making a covenant (David and Jonathan), the context and purpose of that covenant is vastly different than that of marriage. It is not a prescriptive blueprint for marriage but rather a descriptive example of a kingdom-centered friendship in very rare circumstances.[1]

The Holy Spirit continued to convict me as Kelly talked about the dangers of treating friendship like marriage: "It is certainly good to have friends who stick closer than a brother. But it is not good to have friends with whom we are one flesh. Treating a friendship with the weight, exclusivity, and ownership of a marriage is unbiblical and inappropriate. It undermines the institution of marriage and all that marriage points to: the union of Christ and the Church (Eph. 5:31-33)."[2]

After reading *Friend-ish*, I contemplated how I should proceed in my relationship with Avery. Yes, we had fun chatting and hanging out. But as time passed, the dysfunction in our relationship became more and more evident. She also started to become distant. It seemed like she was spending more time with her other friends than with me. She kept putting our relationship on the backburner of her life, which really hurt me—especially because our relationship was such a high priority to me. It felt like she was cheating on me with other girls.

Finally, I made the realization that she was using me—and perhaps always had been.

Partway through my senior year of college, I reflected on the lessons God was teaching me about Avery and my relationship with her: "You're convicting me to be patient and to wait to give my heart to the right guy rather than giving it to Avery in the meantime. I haven't guarded my heart with her. I've tried to substitute our relationship for the romantic relationship I lack. But I think You want me to be 'okay' in this season of lacking."

About two years after I met Avery, our relationship ended in an awkward "breakup" that caused me significant emotional pain. Though we texted a little after my college graduation, we didn't spend much time together after that. I can't even remember the last time I saw her.

Deep down, I never wanted to be "married" to Avery. I wanted to be married to a man who was committed to loving me for his entire life and putting my needs before his own. My efforts to find an equal substitute for marriage resulted in sorrow, not satisfaction.

While I'd love to say Avery was responsible for my pain, that's not completely true. She used me, and she hurt me. She wasn't a very good friend to me. But I never should've tried to substitute our friendship for marriage. Without intending to, I set us up to fail.

Single Girl, only your future husband can truly do something about your innate longing for marriage. None of your friends can. Even your most caring, committed friends can't take your future husband's place.

As you seek to protect your heart while you wait for him, I encourage you to ask yourself the following questions to determine if you're taking your friendships to an unhealthy level:

1. How much time do I spend with my friends?
2. What do I typically talk about with them?
3. How many personal details do I share with them?
4. How intimate (including physically intimate) am I with them?
5. Have the people I trust (like my parents, siblings, pastors, or mentors) expressed any concerns about them?

Nothing is wrong with developing friendships in your season of singleness, but it's important to have the right approach to them. Your friendships—especially your friendships during this season when you're particularly vulnerable—need to have boundaries. In hindsight, I can see that I *didn't* have boundaries in my friendship with Avery. I willingly and consistently played by her rules.

I still have scars from that dysfunctional relationship, but you can avoid the dysfunction (and the scars). Remember that God designed marriage, not friendship, to be the closest relationship between two people—a man and a woman who love each other unconditionally and are committed to staying together until death separates them. Any substitute for that kind of God-ordained, bonded-for-life relationship will be cheap at best and toxic at worst.

//

Amanda's Story

In the Church, singleness is typically viewed as a gift. Single women are sometimes criticized or rebuked for desiring romantic relationships and thus feel guilty about it. But God created humans for relationships, so why shouldn't they desire romantic relationships? This *should* be an acceptable desire, even if He has other things in store for them right now.

The Lord created people for community so that—as the body of Christ—we'll serve alongside one another to glorify Him. All of our relationships should ultimately point toward the gospel. But we must also lay our desire for community—and even our desire for romantic relationships—at the foot of the cross and daily remind ourselves that our Creator and Savior is the only One we'll ever need.

God can mold us to look more like Him through trials or through sweet times of blessing. He can even mold us to look more like Him through our desires for things we can't have yet because it's better for us to wait. So whether we're single or married, let's submit every relationship to Him.

When you fix your eyes on the Lord and how He's working in your life, it doesn't mean having patience and trusting His timing will be easy, but it does mean you'll have significantly more strength as you wait. It also means you'll have more confidence in your purpose. The woman was made to help the man (Gen. 2:18, 20). However, the ultimate purpose of women *and* men is to glorify God—both in singleness and in marriage. So use your season of singleness to be an example to other Christians (1 Tim. 4:12), use your time to bless those in need, and use *all* of your relationships to glorify God.

~Amanda, Single Girl~

Chapter 4

Finding My Future Husband ~~Is~~ Isn't Dependent on Me

Dear Single Girl,

I want to start this chapter by defining an important phrase that I reference multiple times in the pages ahead. The phrase is "intentional socializing." In short, it means resolutely and repeatedly entering social situations (which are often awkward) in order to find love.

Intentional socializing is tiring, but it feels very logical, practical, and executable. I like to believe that me, myself, and I have the whole finding-my-future-husband thing under control. *I* can sign up for the activities. *I* can attend the Bible studies and small groups. *I* can have the conversations.

But me, myself, and I are still single. Though I've put myself out there again and again and again, my efforts haven't resulted in a husband. They haven't even resulted in a boyfriend.

Single Girl, perhaps you've also put yourself out there countless times. You've downloaded various dating apps. You've gone on blind dates. You've tried several churches. You've signed up for mission trips. You've volunteered at community events and local nonprofits. You've attended game nights, movie marathons, and holiday parties hosted by complete strangers. And one thing—your desire to find your future husband—has been the driving force of all the things you've done.

Maybe you feel exhausted from the intentional socializing and disappointed by the lack of results. Maybe you have some doubts about putting yourself out there and wonder if you need to do more. But honestly, doing more isn't always the answer. Connecting with more people, going to more places, and getting involved in more things might not be enough—and believe it or not, that's a very freeing truth.

Love, Grace

I grew up in Maryland, but during my senior year of college, my parents and two sisters (Anna and Jenna) moved from Maryland to Tennessee. When I graduated, I moved in with them and joined them in the "church shopping" process, which was a new experience for me. I attended the same church in Maryland from the year I was born until the year I started college in Tennessee. Even the church I attended during college wasn't a church I had to "shop for" because Anna had been going there long before I joined her at college. I tagged along with her for church and liked it so much that I stayed there until I graduated.

However, my family's move created a unique opportunity for me: the opportunity to find a church. Since I had *zero* success meeting my future husband during college (as I shared in chapter 1), my personal goal was to find a church with lots of eligible bachelors. That goal was surprisingly hard to accomplish though.

For what felt like *centuries*, we visited church after church after church. There were so many churches in our area, which was great. But for one reason or another, we couldn't seem to find a church that felt like a good fit for us—especially for me and my sisters who wanted to attend a church where we *weren't* the youngest members.

Finally, after several discouraging months of searching without success, we found a church we all liked. The worship and teaching were Christ-centered, the people were welcoming, and the college and career group was active. After attending the church for about six months, my sisters and I became members. I felt like I belonged there.

However, I soon began to feel like I didn't *fully* belong there—not because anyone excluded me but because guys and girls in the college and career group started dating, getting engaged, and getting married. It felt like love was in the air—and it lingered in the air for the next few years. Though I faithfully participated in the group with the hope that I'd start dating someone, it became clear that I probably wouldn't. There simply weren't many guys left who were single and near my age. I was thankful for the friendships God provided through the college and career group, but I recognized I needed to go somewhere in *addition* to my home church to do intentional socializing. So I did.

I'm not exaggerating when I say I've been to thirty-one different church groups since my family moved to Tennessee. I've tried young adult Sunday school classes, small groups, Bible studies, and worship gatherings. I attended some groups for one night because I simply couldn't bring myself to return, but I attended other groups for multiple weeks (or even months). I've gone to a variety of places and met a variety of people.

As an introvert who hates entering unfamiliar social situations, I've definitely struggled to walk into new young adult groups knowing I might be rejected. I've encountered far more cliquey girls and passive guys than I thought I would. But the possibility of meeting my future husband has motivated me to persistently put myself out there.

On a few different occasions, I thought I might've met him.

Sam was the first guy who seemed like a great boyfriend possibility for me. I met him at a small group in an older couple's home. I fell for him extremely fast—probably because his personality was extremely stellar. His conversation skills were unlike any I'd encountered from a member of the male species. Apparently his girlfriend thought so too.

Literally on the *third* night Anna and I attended the small group, Sam shared his elaborate proposal plan with us. His girlfriend, who lived in a different state, was in for a real treat. A poem detailing their love story was included in his proposal plan. Needless to say, I was crushed—and emotionally incapable of returning to that small group.

Zane was the next guy I hoped would ask me out. When I initially noticed him at a Bible study, he seemed loud and annoying. He also had an obnoxious crush on the daughter of the couple that led the Bible study.

But when Zane and I started talking after the lesson one night, I began to change my mind about him. He was actually pretty funny and charming. As we chatted, I tried my very best to flirt with him *without* looking or sounding inexperienced.

I quickly developed an obsession with Zane. I looked forward to seeing him at Bible study the next week, but he didn't show up. When he didn't show up the week after that either, I decided to stop going. The disappointment of hoping to see him and not seeing him became too painful for me. And to be honest, most people at that Bible study weren't very friendly.

Fast forward several months (and several intentional socializing opportunities later). I decided to visit a new small group, which met in the leader's apartment. There were only about ten people there, so it didn't take long for me to notice Levi sitting across the room. I was delighted when I saw he wasn't wearing a wedding band because he was quite attractive. When the leader began the lesson, I became even more infatuated with Levi because of the practically perfect things he inserted into the discussion, including his affinity for planning and his desire to be a husband and father. But then he added, "That's about to become a reality because my girlfriend and I designed her engagement ring last week."

Right on cue, disappointment struck. Levi sounded mature, so I guess I shouldn't have been surprised that he had a serious girlfriend—but I was. Knowing he'd be getting married soon, I decided it wouldn't be very wise for me to return to that small group.

I could share several more stories—twenty-eight to be exact—about my intentional socializing efforts and my results, but every story has the same theme: failure. Though I've spent years trying to find love, I haven't found it yet. And I've asked myself this question countless times: *Where could my future husband possibly be?*

Single Girl, you don't need to worry about where your future husband is or question why you haven't found him yet or wonder if you're doing enough to find him. The burden of finding your future husband is a heavy burden to carry—but you don't have to carry it. It's time to stop depending on your own efforts and start depending on the Lord to lead him to you.

//

"The afflicted and needy are seeking water, but there is none,
And their tongue is parched with thirst;
I, the LORD, will answer them Myself,
As the God of Israel I will not forsake them.
"I will open rivers on the bare heights
And springs in the midst of the valleys;
I will make the wilderness a pool of water
And the dry land fountains of water.
"I will put the cedar in the wilderness,
The acacia and the myrtle and the olive tree;
I will place the juniper in the desert
Together with the box tree and the cypress,
That they may see and recognize,
And consider and gain insight as well,
That the hand of the LORD has done this,
And the Holy One of Israel has created it."
(Isa. 41:17-20 NASB)

Though I've desired many things in my life, my "thirst" for a husband is perhaps the most intense desire I've had—probably because it's such a natural human desire, as I talked about in chapter 2. It's basically in my DNA as a woman to crave a loving, committed relationship with a man. I've done my best to seek water to quench this thirst, yet I remain parched.

Honestly, in the process of persistently putting myself out there, I've fallen for the lie that finding my future husband is dependent on me. However, the truth is that it's *not* dependent on me. When I rely on myself to find love instead of relying on God, I place a burden on myself that I wasn't meant to carry. God simply wants me to trust Him. David wrote, "Some trust in chariots and some in horses, but we trust in the name of the LORD our God. They collapse and fall, but we rise and stand upright" (Ps. 20:7-8 ESV).

My pastor once preached a sermon about trusting God's timing using the story of Lazarus from the Gospel of John. After the death of Lazarus, Jesus went to his tomb in Bethany (John 11:1, 38). Lazarus' sisters—Mary and Martha—approached Jesus separately, but both told Him their brother would still be alive if Jesus had been there to prevent his death (John 11:20, 32). Before Lazarus had died, Mary and Martha had sent word to Jesus to alert Him of their brother's illness (John 11:1-3). But Jesus had purposely delayed His trip to Bethany—ultimately because raising Lazarus from the dead would bring Him more glory than healing him from his illness (John 11:4-15, 40-45).

During this sermon, my pastor said God "delays" when He'll be brought more glory from the second outcome than the first outcome. He shared that what might feel like a delay isn't inactivity or idleness. The Lord is always working; He's simply not working based on the timeline I've set for Him.

Single Girl, I realize you might feel pressure to *make* things happen—to go on dates, develop romantic relationships, and ultimately find love. I also realize you might feel helpless when you *can't* make things happen. But there's actually something quite beautiful about helplessness: That's exactly where God meets you.

He meets you when you're looking at the app store on your phone and wondering if the only way you'll meet your future husband is through a dating app. He meets you when you're walking into a young adult Bible study at an unfamiliar church and feeling uncomfortable as you enter a room filled with very affectionate married couples. He meets you when you're stocking shelves at a local food pantry and asking yourself why obnoxious teenagers are the only other people volunteering with you. He meets you when you're driving home from your third blind date this month and holding back tears because not *one* of the guys you've recently met has asked you out on a second date. He meets you when you're boarding a plane for a two-week mission trip to a remote village in the jungle and realizing the handsome teammate you thought was single has actually been married for a decade and has five children.

God meets the helpless in their moments of greatest need and abundantly provides for them. He's fully able to turn a barren wilderness into a luscious forest filled with flowing water so you'll ultimately recognize that His hand—not yours—has done it. In the place where you assume you couldn't possibly meet your future husband, you very well could. The words that Jeremiah prayed long ago—"Nothing is too difficult for You" (Jer. 32:17 NASB)—are true today in your season of singleness.

Before concluding this chapter, I want to clarify a couple specific things. First, I'm *not* saying intentional socializing is a futile endeavor that demonstrates a lack of reliance on God's provision. Real life isn't like *Tangled*. Handsome men don't just stumble upon beautiful women in their secluded areas of the forest. Guys are barely looking for love in their normal surroundings; they're *certainly* not making special trips into the forest to look for it. That's why it's not a good idea to hide away in your house, avoiding any and all social situations.

Second, I'm *not* saying you should pursue guys when you're in social situations with them. You do have a role in finding love, but so does your future husband. It's important to be present and available but not *too* present and available. When you're in a social situation and a guy catches your eye, let him come to you. Let him engage you in conversation. Let him ask for your number. Let him text or call you first. If he's interested in getting to know you, he will.

While it's important to participate in God's plan by taking steps to find love, there's only so much you can do—and that's all you need to do. If you're tired of putting yourself out there and getting rejected, don't be discouraged. This isn't about you; it's about God's ability to turn what feels like a desert wasteland into a tropical paradise. The helpless can find rest in their powerful Provider.

//

Susan's Story

I was single until I was thirty-five. When I was young, energetic, and available—in my prime—I worked as a volunteer coordinator and development director at a Christian homeless shelter. Outside work, I served children in church ministries, spent time with single and married friends, traveled, read biographies of Christians (including lifelong single female missionaries), and hosted people in my home.

Throughout my single years, I desired to be married. I read books on marriage and listened to Christian radio discussions about it. I loved going to my friends' weddings and spending time with my brother's children. I often hoped for marriage and wondered if I'd experience it.

But I also recognized the significance of contentment. In his first letter to Timothy, Paul wrote, "But godliness actually is a means of great gain when accompanied by contentment" (1 Tim. 6:6 NASB). This is true for our whole lives and pertains to our relationship status, as well as our possessions. Thus, I encourage single women today to be content with what—and whom—God has given them.

Seek God's kingdom first in every area of your life (Matt. 6:33). Serve Him by patiently serving those He's placed around you. Study Proverbs 31, Titus 2, and biographies of godly women. Remember the person you are now is the person you'll be when you're married, so focus more on *becoming* the right person than *finding* the right person.

Maintain biblically high standards for the kind of man you want to marry. Refuse to settle. When you become interested in a guy, observe how he treats people in need, as well as how he treats his family members and friends. If you live for eternal things and seek God's kingdom first, you'll find yourself in the company of others doing the same.

~Susan, Former Single Girl~

Chapter 5

Being Single ~~Does~~ Doesn't Mean I'm Behind

Dear Single Girl,

Not long ago, I scrolled through the contacts on my phone. It ended up being a very depressing activity because I realized how many married girls I knew and how few single girls I knew. Suddenly, I felt like the exception rather than the rule.

Initially, the transition from having mostly single friends to having mostly married friends seemed gradual. I can remember the first wedding I attended where one of my friends (rather than one of my babysitters) was the bride. I was eighteen, and she was nineteen. As one of her bridesmaids, I wore a mint green dress and white wedge heels, got my hair and nails done, and walked down the beach with a bouquet in hand to stand beside her during the ceremony.

In a way, that wedding was my introduction to singleness. A small number of my friends got married during my college years, but when I finished college, everything changed. Nothing felt gradual anymore—except my own journey to find love. Frankly, the kids I once babysat or watched in the church nursery will probably get married before I do. I just have an eerie feeling that I'll still be single several years from now—maybe even a decade or two from now.

Single Girl, do you have that eerie feeling too? You probably didn't expect to be in this situation. You thought your season of singleness would be short and sweet, not long and miserable. You were confident you'd have a husband and at least two kids by now.

Yet here you are. No kids. No husband. Not even a boyfriend. Getting older with each passing day and genuinely starting to believe you might be alone forever.

Before you start to panic, I want you to remember something: Even if you *feel* behind, you *aren't* behind. The Lord's plan for each person is unique, so there's really no such thing as "behind." I promise He's working behind the scenes, orchestrating the timing that's perfect for you and your future husband.

Love, Grace

The first couple years after I graduated from college were unexpectedly challenging. As I shared in chapter 4, I began attending a church where romantic relationships were blossoming, especially among the young adults in the college and career group. Sometimes it was discouraging to attend a church where I didn't know many people—and where the few people I *did* know were dating, getting engaged, and getting married.

Don't get me wrong—the people at my church were (and are) good people who didn't reject me because I was new or because I was single. But *not* being in a romantic relationship still made me feel left out. I felt like I couldn't fully connect with my friends there because most of them had something I was missing.

I had to accept my awkward stage of being finished with college but not yet having a husband or a fiancé or even a boyfriend. I was no longer a college student surrounded by tons of guys who could become my future husband. Nor was I a married woman enveloped by the love of my husband and able to start a family. And I struggled to appreciate that in-between stage of life.

Since I'm not a college student and I'm not a wife, who am I? I wondered. *Is there anyone else who has to live in this awkward in-between stage? There certainly don't seem to be many eligible bachelors in it.*

The awkward in-between stage felt even more awkward upon the arrival of 2022 (which I refer to as "the year everyone else found love"). It's possible that some engagements and weddings happened in 2022 because COVID-19 had delayed people's romantic plans in 2020 and 2021. But deep down, I knew I was simply at the age when many of my peers were ready to tie the knot and had found people with whom to tie it.

Our fridge quickly filled up with save-the-dates and wedding invitations for family members and friends. Wedding #1 was in May, wedding #2 was in June, and wedding #3 was in July. Unfortunately, I had to miss wedding #4 in July, wedding #5 in August, and wedding

#6 in December due to distance. But I was hopeful that my future husband would be at *one* of the weddings I planned to attend.

At wedding #1, I watched the incredibly passionate kiss of the bride and groom, ate pancakes and bacon as I made small talk with people from my church, and wondered why the groomsman who clearly didn't have anyone to dance with wasn't asking *me* to dance. I honestly felt discouraged about getting so dolled up and not meeting anyone special at the ceremony or reception.

When I didn't meet a *single* single guy at wedding #1, I decided to pray I'd meet a guy at wedding #2. I figured it didn't hurt to ask (okay, *plead*) for God to bring a guy into my life via that wedding. And He did—but I failed to appreciate the guy He provided.

I met Harrison at wedding #2. He was single, and he seemed nice. He was definitely attentive to me. Unfortunately, though, *I* wasn't very attentive to *him*. Honestly, I wasn't really attracted to Harrison—plus, I was too distracted by all the couples in attendance to hear anything he said throughout the evening. Poor Harrison.

Wedding #3 was also a bust. Though I *saw* plenty of guys I was interested in meeting, I guess *they* weren't interested in meeting *me*. What a bummer.

In 2023, I attended a February wedding, an August wedding, and a September wedding. The August and September weddings were lovely, but absolutely nothing romantic happened to me at either of them. However, the February wedding was different.

I'd watched the beautiful love story of the bride and groom unfold over the course of several months. They were good friends of mine. Although I definitely wanted to meet a guy at their wedding, I didn't really expect to because it sounded like most people on the guest list were married.

But then I met Jonathan.

At the reception, each guest was assigned to a specific table, and Jonathan was assigned to the same table as me and my sisters. We were at our table talking when he sat down, and I honestly expected him to ignore us. Instead, he struck up a conversation with us. I was immediately impressed—and incredibly distracted by his intense blue eyes, which were practically *begging* me to get lost in them.

Jonathan—a childhood friend of the groom—was interesting, kind, and handsome. I discovered that he'd been homeschooled and studied business in college. I also found out that he served in the military and lived in Colorado. Unfortunately, I didn't learn much more about him because the reception was so loud that I could barely hear him. But I didn't mind too much. I just soaked him in as I smiled and tried to insert something amusing into the conversation every now and then.

After the meal had been served and the speeches had been given, I headed over to the dance floor and started to boogie (which was challenging because I'm an absolutely terrible dancer). I danced to the "Cupid Shuffle" and the "Cha Cha Slide" among many other songs. I made a graceful exit to my seat for the slow songs and promptly returned to the dance floor when the hype songs started to play again.

Then I caught Jonathan staring at me from the other side of the dance floor.

Jonathan, please *ask me to dance,* I thought. *Or at least ask for my number before I leave because you live on the other side of the country and I might never see you again.*

What happened next is the same thing that always happens: nothing. After the wedding, I learned Jonathan had a girlfriend. (A true shocker, I know.)

And right on cue, worst-case scenarios flooded into my mind: *What if singleness truly is my fate? What if I never have a boyfriend? What if I never get married? What if I never hold a guy's hand or have my first kiss or have sex? Is there a solid guy somewhere out there for me, or am I wasting my time hoping that he exists? Why does it feel like everyone has found love except me?*

Let's fast forward to the beginning of 2024. Even though a year had passed since I'd met Jonathan, I hadn't stopped thinking about him. Deep down, I wanted him to break up with his girlfriend and fall in love with me.

When I found out Jonathan would be visiting my friends during their one-year anniversary weekend, I dared to dream.

This could be my chance, I thought. *When Jonathan sees me again, he'll realize he's been dating the wrong girl all this time. He'll see he belongs with me!*

A couple days before Jonathan's arrival, I lifted up this desperate prayer: "Dear God, *please* let Jonathan be single when he visits my friends this weekend. And *please* let him be interested in me. I know Your will is best. I just pray You'll make this happen because I can't; only You can."

I was absolutely delighted when I saw Jonathan at church two days later and he wasn't with his girlfriend. I wondered if they'd broken up. I felt hopeful that a beautiful romance between me and Jonathan would soon begin.

But when I saw him later that day at a church gathering and there was a girl—*his* girl—standing next to him, my hopefulness vanished instantly.

"This is Jonathan," my friends said—as if I hadn't remembered his name, his charming smile, or his gorgeous eyes.

"I think we met at the wedding," Jonathan piped up.

"Yeah, I think you're right!" I said, faking forgetfulness.

Throughout the event that night, I continued faking forgetfulness—pretending I hadn't spent the past year thinking about Jonathan or wanting him to break up with his girlfriend—to conceal my sheer disappointment. But I could only force smiles and laughter for a little while. Despair set in as I went home.

There aren't any good guys left, I thought. *I'll never find love. I'm going to be alone forever.*

Single Girl, you might expect this story to have a Hallmark-esque ending, but honestly, it doesn't. I didn't run into a handsome stranger as I left the event, discover he was even more charming than Jonathan, and marry him the following year. Something better happened though: I remembered I wasn't forgotten.

> I waited patiently for the LORD;
>
> And He inclined to me and heard my cry.
>
> He brought me up out of the pit of destruction, out of the miry clay,
>
> And He set my feet upon a rock making my footsteps firm.

He put a new song in my mouth, a song of praise to our God;
Many will see and fear
And will trust in the LORD.

How blessed is the man who has made the LORD his trust,
And has not turned to the proud, nor to those who lapse into falsehood.
Many, O LORD my God, are the wonders which You have done,
And Your thoughts toward us;
There is none to compare with You.
If I would declare and speak of them,
They would be too numerous to count.
(Ps. 40:1-5 NASB)

My relationship with Jonathan (if you can even call it that, ahem) felt like a rollercoaster of emotions—from enchantment to denial to excitement to disappointment. But as days turned into weeks and weeks turned into months, I slowly began to release my desire to have him. I was done begging God to make him mine because it was clear he wasn't meant to be mine. Still, knowing that Jonathan wasn't meant for me was a difficult reality to accept. I tried to take David's approach to prayer to deal with my discouragement.

About two months after Jonathan's visit, during my quiet time on a Wednesday morning, I decided not to ask God to give me Jonathan. Instead, I simply poured out my heart, telling Him I missed Jonathan and wished we had a shot at a relationship. I wrote, "I'm not going to ask You to make it happen . . . but my heart hurts a little as I think about [me] not being his and him not being mine."

Honestly, I sometimes struggle with doubts about prayer, worrying that God doesn't hear me when I pray. But on that particular morning, I decided to thank God for hearing me. Then I finished my quiet time and started my workday.

Just a few hours later, the Lord answered my prayer—not by responding in an audible voice but by sending me a guy.

I noticed the guy while I was working from my favorite coffee shop. As I was working (and people-watching), I saw him enter the coffee shop and sit down with an older man at a table near mine. Though I wasn't particularly intrigued by the guy at first, my ears perked up as he started sharing his life story with the older man. Over the course of an hour, I learned a great deal about him.

He was twenty-eight. He had a dad, a mom, a sister, a brother-in-law, and a niece. He worked as a nurse in the intensive care unit at a local hospital. He enjoyed traveling, playing tennis, and making to-do lists. He liked going to the gym, but he wasn't obsessed with it.

He became a Christian when he was thirteen. He left his previous church because he didn't feel like he was growing there. But he found another church, and he served as a greeter and a small group leader for sixth-grade boys.

He was ready to get married. He wanted to have a family. He'd only had two serious girlfriends in his life. He wasn't a fan of dating apps.

He didn't have any tattoos, piercings, or weird facial hair. His clothes were trendy but not *too* trendy. He was cute. Very cute.

As their conversation came to a close, the older man (who I discovered was the guy's new mentor) asked the guy how he could be praying for him. The guy shared his prayer requests. Then he asked the older man, “Is there any way I can be praying for you?”

Tears instantly welled up in my eyes. I didn’t even know this guy personally, but he genuinely felt like proof—proof that godly single guys really exist, proof that my future husband really exists, and proof that the Lord really hears me when I pour out my heart to Him. I believe God placed him in my life to remind me, “Grace, I have someone for you—someone like Jonathan but better. I have someone for you who will love you the way you love him.” And more importantly, I believe God placed him in my life to remind me, “I haven’t forgotten you.”

It’s so easy to feel forgotten when our friends enter seasons of life that we’re not in yet—like engagement and marriage—because they’re moving on and we’re not. But remembering that we’re not forgotten can change the way we view our season of singleness. If I’d remembered God’s goodness during the Jonathan situation, I probably wouldn’t have fallen into despair—but even when I fell, He saved me “out of the miry clay” and “set my feet upon a rock,” just as David declared in Psalm 40:2 (NASB).

Even when despair feels like our only option, we can choose to have hope instead, as Jeremiah described in this powerful passage:

> This I recall to my mind,
> Therefore I have hope.
> The LORD’s lovingkindnesses indeed never cease,
> For His compassions never fail.
> They are new every morning;
> Great is Your faithfulness.
> “The LORD is my portion,” says my soul,

> "Therefore I have hope in Him."
>
> The LORD is good to those who wait for Him,
>
> To the person who seeks Him.
>
> It is good that he waits silently
>
> For the salvation of the LORD.
>
> (Lam. 3:21-26 NASB)

Unfortunately, despair—rather than remembrance—is normally my first response when I face something difficult. Instead of pausing to consider God's presence and promises, I allow worst-case scenarios to consume me. It's only when I wait silently—not despairingly—for God to act, recall His love toward me, and rely on Him completely that I can have true hope.

Single Girl, what's your initial response when hard things happen as you're waiting for marriage? Where do you turn when you realize the guy who once loved you no longer does? How do you process the news of a potential suitor deciding to date someone else? What is your reaction when yet another one of your friends gets engaged? Do you allow doubt and discouragement to consume you? Or do you pause to remember the truth that you aren't forsaken or forgotten?

If you don't continually entrust your fears to God, they'll control you—and you can't let them. The unknowns in your life are known to God, so there's no need to be apprehensive. Before you start to panic about the future, ponder how He's worked in the past and how He's working in the present. Silence the lie that He's working in your friends' lives but not in yours. There's no such thing as "behind" in His plan; every part of it is perfectly timed.

If you tried to count every thought God has toward you and every wonder He's doing in your life, you wouldn't be able to add them up. There are *endless* ways He has worked, is working, and will work. So on the days when you're tempted to despair, don't forget to remember.

//

Abbie's Story

I think singleness is often viewed as a temporary season of suffering that everyone experiences. For many people I know, this season ended quickly. But when you're still single in your late twenties and you're watching everyone around you get married and have children, it's easy to feel like you're the only single person left on the planet. Singleness can feel like a chapter you simply need to skip through in order to truly begin your life.

To be honest, I've struggled with that feeling for a long time. But recently, the Lord has taught me that it's not just the *next* season that will allow me to live out His calling for my life; it's *this* season too. I can actually start living my life now instead of dwelling on the next season of life (which is something I'm so guilty of doing).

Starting to live life *now* sounds so simple, but actually doing it is hard. I have to continually take my desire for marriage to the feet of Jesus and ask Him to change my discouragement to excitement for each and every season of life. I have to practice this daily because it's so easy to lose sight of the truth. I have to remind myself that feeling behind isn't a struggle that's restricted to a particular season of life. We'll always have feelings of discontentment if we aren't focused on the right thing: our relationships with the Lord. He can use any season to sanctify us, not just the seasons of marriage and motherhood. Though there are specific lessons we can learn during those future seasons, it doesn't mean we aren't worthy to enjoy life until we reach them.

If you find yourself in a season similar to mine, take your struggles to Jesus. Lay them at His feet and learn to live for today. The weight of this world isn't meant to be carried alone because we aren't strong enough to do that. We'll fail every single time we try to take the reins of control.

Following the Lord and choosing to let Him lead our lives is a daily decision (Luke 9:23). So whenever you feel yourself slip into worry, give Him your concerns (1 Pet. 5:7). Surrender control, be thankful for where He has you in this moment, and know you're never alone.

~Abbie, Single Girl~

Chapter 6

Settling ~~Is~~ Isn't My Only Option

Dear Single Girl,

When I was about thirteen, I made a list of qualities I wanted my future husband to have. I don't remember everything I included on my list, and I don't know if I'll ever see it again because it's probably tucked away in a storage bin. But if I had to guess, my list was likely very long and very full of cliché things like "honest" and "kind."

Frankly, I didn't have the right mindset when I made my list. I assumed that meeting a guy with all the qualities on it would be easy. However, at some point between making that list and writing this book, I realized it was much easier to record those qualities than to actually meet a guy who possesses them.

Single Girl, I'm guessing you've found the same thing to be true because you're reading this book. Perhaps you made a list several years ago with every quality you wanted your future husband to have. Though you did include some superficial things on your list, your top priority was his commitment to Jesus. Since then, however, you've discovered that guys who share your faith are few and far between, and now you wonder if you shouldn't have bothered to make that list. After all, it's only caused you to develop unrealistically high expectations for your future husband. The guy from your list probably doesn't even exist in reality. If you just lowered your standards a little, you could be dating, engaged, and married within a year.

I understand how appealing that might sound. But this isn't the time to settle; it's the time to pray like you've never prayed before. You haven't waited for your future husband for this long to give in or give up now. If marriage is part of God's plan for you, He'll provide a guy who follows Him—and he'll be worth waiting for. Your responsibility is simple: Wait for him.

Love, Grace

Soon after I started my first post-college job, I realized I needed to find a different job because my work situation was toxic. It was a stressful time in my life, but thankfully, I only ended up being unemployed for a few days. As I applied for various positions, God provided several interviews, which encouraged me in my job search and ultimately led me to the point where I had to choose which job opportunity to pursue.

Honestly, I knew I wanted the job at the technology consulting company as soon as I walked into the conference room for the interview and met a guy named Tate with dark hair and eyes. I was already nervous about the interview, but meeting him took me to a whole new level of nervousness. Though I maintained my composure throughout the interview, I almost lost it when the interview ended and he opened the door for me on my way out. Needless to say, I was *thrilled* when that company offered me a job.

On my first day, I discovered I was going to work in a room with Tate, which pleased me immensely. But frankly, being three feet away from him made it difficult for me to focus on my tasks. His presence was quite distracting—especially while he was training me. As he explained various things to me, my mind wandered. All I could think about was his deep voice and sharp jawline.

It felt like there was a magnet pulling me toward him. I couldn't figure out why I was so smitten with him. I mean, I appreciated his confidence. He was suave and charming. I liked his wavy hair, adorable smile, and spot-on fashion sense. His swag was probably the best thing about him.

The *worst* thing about him was his lack of a relationship with Jesus.

Tate never directly said he wasn't a Christian, but honestly, he didn't have to. I could just tell. It didn't take long for me to see that we didn't have the same priorities in life.

During my first week of work, I went out to lunch with some of my coworkers, including Tate. At lunch, I asked about fun local activities because my family was still new to the area at the time. I found it pretty concerning that he responded by asking, "Do you drink?"

That wasn't the only time I noticed Tate's *passion* for alcohol. On my way out the door after work one day, I saw him drinking whiskey—not sparkling grape juice, unfortunately—while he was in the office. I tried to brush it off, but forgetting about it was hard. Apparently, he needed alcohol so badly he couldn't even wait until after he left the office to consume it.

On top of that, profanities seemed to fly out of Tate's mouth whenever he got annoyed.

Though it was clear that Tate and I had little in common, I still liked him. I still got nervous when he was around, I still enjoyed interacting with him, and I still wanted him to ask me out. Even after I invited him to church for Easter and he essentially told me that church wasn't his thing, I still had a huge crush on him.

There was really only one thing that kept me and Tate from going out (and it wasn't his lack of a relationship with Jesus): He wasn't romantically interested in me. He simply viewed me as a coworker. In fact, he became more and more distant over time.

During my first several weeks at the company, Tate and I worked in the same room, just a few feet away from each other. Within a couple months of my start date, he moved to a different room in our office. He then started working from home more often. And less than a year after I joined the company, he began working remotely almost every day of the week. I rarely saw him anymore.

What did I do to scare him away? I wondered. *Why did he work in the office when I first started this job but then switch to working remotely? Was he intrigued by me initially but then realized I'm a goody-two-shoes who doesn't have anything in common with him?*

There was zero chemistry between me and Tate. We were barely friends and definitely nothing more than that. I hardly knew anything about him, so our interactions were very impersonal. The extent of our typical conversation was "hello" and/or "goodbye." If I was lucky, I'd get a quick "How are you?" from him during one of his infrequent trips to the office.

Early into my job, I figured out that Tate liked a girl named Tessa. She worked at our company. Although he never admitted that he liked her, it was obvious that he did.

I hadn't met Tessa in person because she only worked remotely, but everyone—including Tate—raved about her intelligence. One day, he literally called her a "data goddess," which was a major blow to my confidence. Even though it felt like I did way more of Tate's grunt work than Tessa did, he didn't praise me nearly as much as he praised her. He talked about how funny and smart she was, but he never told me how funny or smart (or beautiful, hello?) I was. To him, I was just a "resource." He irked me when he failed to commend my diligence.

When the day of the company Christmas party arrived, I actually felt relieved that I wouldn't be able to attend because I knew that Tessa would be there—and that Tate would be flirting with her. Eventually, I did meet the infamous "data goddess," but I was rather unimpressed. Though she seemed nice, she didn't really strike me as a goddess.

Despite Tate's obvious disinterest in me (and his very obvious interest in Tessa), my attraction to him was intense.

Why do I want to go out with this non-Christian guy whom I barely know anything about? I asked myself. *Why do I daydream about him? Why do I even* like *him?*

I don't really know what made Tate so irresistible to me. After all, he wasn't a Christian, he had several unhealthy habits, and he didn't treat me with respect. Thankfully, God knew I was better off without him—even though *I* didn't know that yet.

Single Girl, I know it might not seem like a big deal to have a crush on a non-Christian guy. After all, it's not like you're marrying him. Plus, he could change his mind about Jesus. He could start going to church with you, decide to follow Jesus, and even become a great spiritual leader. But what if he doesn't? Those are all *possibilities*, not *guarantees*. It's equally likely (if not *more* likely) that he won't become a Christian. Though God could do a miracle in his life one day, I recommend you move on before you become as attached to him as I became to Tate.

//

> Now King Solomon loved many foreign women along with the daughter of Pharaoh: Moabite, Ammonite, Edomite, Sidonian, and Hittite women, from the nations concerning which the LORD had said to the sons of Israel, "You shall not associate with them, nor shall they associate with you, for they will surely turn your heart away after their gods." Solomon held fast to these in love. He had seven hundred wives, princesses, and three hundred concubines, and his wives turned his heart away. For when Solomon was old, his wives turned his heart away after other gods; and his heart was not wholly devoted to the LORD God, as the heart of David his father had been. For Solomon went after Ashtoreth the goddess of the Sidonians and after Milcom the detestable idol of the Ammonites. Solomon did what was evil in the sight of the LORD, and did not follow the LORD fully, as David his father had done. Then Solomon built a high place for Chemosh the detestable idol of Moab, on the mountain which is east of Jerusalem, and for Molech the detestable idol of the sons of Ammon. Thus also he did for all his foreign wives, who burned incense and sacrificed to their gods. (1 Kings 11:1-8 NASB)

To be honest, Solomon's life saddens me because his reign as king of Israel had such a promising start but such a disappointing end. After David died and Solomon took his place, God appeared to him in a dream and told him to ask for whatever he wanted, and he humbly asked for an understanding heart so he could judge the Israelites with discernment (1 Kings 3:5-9; 2 Chron. 1:7-10). God found pleasure in Solomon's request, so He not only promised him wisdom—beyond the wisdom of any other king who had lived or would live—but also promised him wealth and honor (1 Kings 3:10-14; 2 Chron. 1:11-12). For a time, the kingdom flourished—and so did Solomon.

The Lord later appeared to Solomon again, warning him about the consequences of turning away from Him (1 Kings 9:1-9; 2 Chron. 7:12-22). But rather than heeding God's warning, Solomon dove head-first into sin. He married 700 women, and they worshipped many different gods and led him astray (1 Kings 11:1-8). His choice to hold fast to women who didn't worship God had significant consequences. Solomon's family lost the kingdom—except two tribes, Benjamin and Judah—to Solomon's servant (1 Kings 11:11-13, 11:26-39, 12:15-24; 2 Chron. 10:15-11:4). Sadly, Solomon's love for pagan women tainted his entire life and legacy.

In His kindness, the Lord spared me from a romantic relationship with Tate that likely would've wrecked every other relationship in my life—including my relationship with Him. Yes, sometimes Tate's lack of attraction to me *felt* like a curse. But in reality, it was a blessing.

During the nearly two years I worked for the technology consulting company, there was really only one time when Tate actually seemed to like me the way I liked him. We were at TopGolf for a work event, and we were on the same team. Our objective was to score the most points by hitting the golf ball toward the target areas on the green.

A few months before that event, Tessa had left the company, so it was actually pretty fun to hang out with Tate. He didn't mention the "data goddess" at all that night. Even though it was dumb luck, I golfed super well—which not only helped my team earn several points but also caused Tate to give me a lot of attention.

I'm not exactly sure what made him so attentive to me at the event. It could've been the alcohol he was consuming or the tight pants I was wearing. Or it could've solely been the unprecedented golf skills I was exhibiting that night (and *only* that night, unfortunately).

I'll probably remember that night for years to come—not because I golfed so well or because I received so much attention from Tate but because I was so focused on someone who was so wrong for me. I'd been a Christian for almost my entire life, yet I was willing to settle for a non-Christian guy who shared none of my beliefs or values. I was willing to give up everything for an alcoholic with a dirty mouth and a conceited attitude who wanted nothing to do with my Creator and Savior. He was *far, far less* than God's best for me.

Over time, I did become less interested in Tate. I ended up leaving the company to take a job at a Christian ministry. Tate stayed. As far as I know, he still works there.

However, a few weeks before I left, God let me see how Tate saw me—not romantically but still positively. Frankly, I wasn't a great example to Tate of how a Christian should live. But I watched God graciously redeem the situation.

Shortly before my last day at the company, I helped train a new employee. As I was explaining my job to her, I noticed a message from Tate pop up on her computer that said, "Enjoy your training with Grace! She really knows her stuff." I was touched.

A couple days later, Tate asked me about speaking at a weekly meeting he held with some team members outside my department. He wanted me to share a few insights about my role with them. Though it probably meant nothing to him, it meant a lot to me.

After the meeting, Tate messaged me to thank me for sharing and let me know I'd be missed at the company. When I explained I'd be transitioning to a position at a ministry, he said, "I'm really happy to hear that. . . . I know that's what [you're] passionate about, and it's great you get to immerse yourself in it." His encouragement pleasantly surprised me.

The weeks leading up to my last day at the company were full of lightbulb moments—and it felt like God was saying, "Even though Tate doesn't see you romantically, he sees you exactly how I want him to see you."

After many, many months of hoping Tate would view me in a romantic way, I finally realized his lack of attraction to me was a *good* thing. And it was a relief to know he appreciated my work ethic and understood where my heart lay. He could tell I cared about doing a good job and wanted to use my skills in a ministry role. That was enough for me.

Single Girl, that's enough for you too. Though it might be hard to release your desire for a romantic relationship with a guy who isn't a Christian, it'll be much easier to release it now than to face the consequences of hanging on to it. God *isn't* heartless, but He *is* holy. He graciously warns you about the dangers of becoming attached to those who don't share your faith because He wants to protect you. No matter how many great things you do for God in your life, holding fast to a non-Christian can taint your entire life and legacy, just like it did to Solomon's.

Yes, it's important to shine God's light to everyone you encounter, including your non-Christian crush, but your light—not your heart—is exactly what he needs. I promise that settling for him isn't your only option. The alternative is harder, but it's far more rewarding. If you're willing to wait for a guy who follows Jesus, you might be surprised by how many other qualities he has from your list.

//

Natalie's Story

Growing up in a Christian environment, I always expected to end up with a guy who loved Jesus more than he loved me, had a sparkling personality, and wanted to raise a godly family. Many ideas *also* entered my head as a result of watching way too many Hallmark movies—like experiencing love at first sight as the heavens opened up and rays of light shone down on my Prince Charming. I genuinely thought a ring by spring, a romantic proposal, and a wedding right after my college graduation were all desires God would fulfill. But reality looked a little different.

During the first couple years after college, God showed me how to see Him as my first love and gave me confidence in my singleness, but there was still a desire in my heart to meet my future husband and share my life with him.

I moved back into my parents' house with no husband and no prospects. But when I started a new job, I started receiving special attention from one of my coworkers. He was intentional and friendly, and he seemed eager to learn more about me. Anxiety lingered in my heart as I accepted his invitation to lunch. I tried to silence my fears by telling myself that he was just a friend and that we might have fun together.

On that first date, I talked about my love for Jesus to see if he shared my feelings. Although he seemed interested in what I said, he looked at me as if I were speaking in a foreign language. I thought that we'd simply continue to share the same workplace and that things wouldn't go any further between us.

However, he continued to pursue me, and I honestly enjoyed it. Having someone to talk to and spend time with was fun, and he treated me like a princess. Even though I prayed about our relationship, I still felt so torn about it. Something felt off.

Between my family's concerns about our relationship and my own anxiety about it, my then-boyfriend and I reached a breaking point. I knew deep down that we weren't heading the same direction in life. Though he desperately tried to fit into the "Christian" box for me, it just resulted in both of us feeling hurt and confused.

When I finally ended the relationship, my mom told me, "I bet you'll be engaged to someone else in a year." I laughed and told her there was no way that would happen because I wasn't going to date for at *least* two years. I'm so glad I was wrong though. I met my husband a few months after that breakup, got engaged a year later, and got married a few months after that. My husband loves Jesus more than he loves me, has a sparkling personality, and wants to raise a godly family. God truly uses all parts of our stories for His perfect plan.

~Natalie, Former Single Girl~

Chapter 7

Yellow Flags ~~Are~~ Aren't Trivial

Dear Single Girl,

The current version of this chapter is quite different from the original version. I actually wrote the original version before I had any dating experience. Until March 2025, my reality was unrequited love—liking guys who didn't like me in return—so this chapter was based on my observations of others' romantic relationships, not my own experiences. But then a guy named James entered my life and forever changed my perspective on yellow flags.

Everyone seems to talk about red flags—the glaring issues in romantic relationships, like when Christians date non-Christians (as I discussed in chapter 6). However, no one seems to talk about yellow flags. To be honest, the topic of yellow flags became much more difficult but much more necessary for me to write about after dating a guy who had them. They're not as big and bold as red flags, but they're just as important to look out for.

The yellow flags I saw in James made me feel uneasy—and I believe that feeling came from the Lord. Though he wasn't a *terrible* guy, he wasn't the *right* guy. After we stopped dating, I realized he wasn't even a *good* guy.

Single Girl, I realize red flags are easier to spot and heed than yellow flags, but my hope is that you'll pay attention to both, even when you're tempted to ignore them. Frankly, the things that cause you to pause when you're dating probably won't disappear when you're married. If you doubt that someone is the right guy for you, he probably isn't.

Compatibility, commitment, and character are three essential things you'll see in the right guy. Yes, he'll have flaws, but that's not a reason to settle for someone else while you wait for him to enter your life. Trust me—it's not worth it.

Love, Grace

I connected with James through a series of events that felt like crazy coincidences (though in chapter 9, I'll explain why they weren't). I met him at a mixer for Christian singles in a coffee shop. When I walked into the coffee shop, I brought extremely low expectations with me. I assumed I'd see a dozen girls and a couple guys and then suffer through two hours of small talk with them. Although small talk *was* a key part of the event, my first assumption turned out to be totally wrong. Nearly seventy people were crammed into the coffee shop.

Soon after I arrived, the "mingle bingo" began. Each square on the bingo card had a specific characteristic on it—for example, "aunt or uncle." To mark off that square, I had to find someone who was an aunt or an uncle.

Throughout the next hour, I chatted with several guys, but none stood out to me—until Jenna introduced me to a tall, dark, and handsome guy with kind eyes and an earnest smile.

"Hi, I'm James," he said.

"Hi, I'm Grace," I said. "Are you the James who's left-handed?" I'd heard multiple people mention a left-handed guy named James, and I hadn't been able to mark off the "left-handed" square on my bingo card yet.

"I'm actually ambidextrous," he answered. I felt like ambidextrous *definitely* counted.

By the time I met James, the mixer was almost over—but I was smitten with him instantly. I actually enjoyed small-talking with him, and he actually seemed to enjoy small-talking with me. I felt like we hit it off, so I was disappointed that he didn't ask for my number. Still, I knew God would make a way for me to see him again if it was His will.

I saw him again two weeks later.

Some people from the mixer got together to play pickleball on a Saturday morning. Butterflies fluttered around my stomach as I entered the building and spotted James on the court. To my delight, I got paired up with him. When one of the guys in the group noted how well James and I complemented each other on the court, the number of butterflies in my stomach doubled.

Our group played several two-on-two games of pickleball that morning. After a couple hours, everyone headed to a nearby restaurant. I noticed James was quiet during lunch, but I enjoyed simply sitting across from him. When everyone finished eating and I stood up to leave the restaurant, he piped up, "Grace! Would you mind if I got your number?"

My heart skipped a beat—or maybe a dozen. When I told him I wouldn't mind, a stupid grin spread across my face, which probably revealed I hadn't heard such a question before. I happily put my number in his phone and then headed home.

Later that day, James texted to ask if I was interested in getting coffee. Reading his text was a euphoric experience because no one had ever asked me out before. I excitedly texted back to say yes, and he suggested a specific day and place. He asked what time would work best with my schedule, and we agreed to meet at a local coffee shop on the upcoming Friday afternoon. It couldn't come soon enough.

I can't believe a guy I like actually likes me back! I thought gleefully. *He was brave enough to ask for my number and ask me out. I'm finally going to go on my first date!*

For the next six days, thoughts about what had happened—and what *could* happen—with James filled my mind.

On Thursday, he texted to confirm that we were still going to meet the next day. He also suggested bringing a jacket so we could walk at the park near the coffee shop if I was interested. (I was *definitely* interested.)

When I arrived at the coffee shop on Friday afternoon, James was already inside, sitting at a table with an iced chai tea latte. I walked up to his table and greeted him. We hugged. Then he told me, "You can go ahead and order if you want."

Uh, you're not going to buy my coffee? I thought, caught off-guard. *That's pretty lame.*

Attempting to conceal my disbelief, I made my way to the counter and ordered myself an iced mocha latte. With drinks in hand, James and I started walking to the park and sat down on a bench to talk. As we talked, I noticed him scooting closer and closer to me on the bench—and I momentarily forgot why I was irritated with him. When I raised my arm to tuck my hair behind my ear, my arm brushed against his. The number of butterflies in my stomach doubled yet again.

Even though I was nervous, I attempted to stay engaged throughout our date. James told me about various aspects of his life, including his job, his church, and his family. He talked about staying active and spending time outside. He shared why he moved to Tennessee.

Honestly, though, I struggled to follow his train of thought during much of our date. He seemed distracted—as if he were somewhere far, far away. Plus, he hardly asked me any questions, and the questions he did ask me felt pretty frivolous. He asked about my opinion on playing and watching sports, and he wanted to know how I stayed physically active. My all-time favorite moment of the date was when he brought up a "serious girlfriend" from the not-too-distant past.

Needless to say, I felt perplexed and annoyed after date #1.

Why did James even ask me out? I wondered. *I don't think he had a good time. He seemed oddly unengaged. He wasn't flirty or funny or complimentary. I doubt he'll ever ask me out again.*

Several hours later, however, he texted to say, "I really enjoyed hanging out with you today—I hope you had a great time." I considered responding by saying, "Well, I don't believe you." But instead, I simply echoed what he said.

Two days later, he texted to ask if I was interested in meeting at a farmers market on the upcoming Saturday morning. His text literally said, "I have something going on during the day on Saturday, but [I] could meet up for an hour when it opens at 8:30." I was tempted to send a snarky reply—something like "Are you sure you can spare one hour of your week for me? I'd hate to take up any of your very precious time." But instead, I told him I was interested—and then I nervously anticipated Saturday's arrival.

My nervousness intensified when I found out the farmers market wouldn't be open on the upcoming Saturday due to limited off-season hours. But I didn't mention that to James. I wanted to let him handle the situation and figure out a plan B—especially because he didn't strike me as a plan B kind of guy.

James' original plan for date #2 was for us to meet at a coffee shop near the farmers market and then walk over together. At 6:30 a.m. on Saturday—two hours before we were scheduled to meet—he let me know that he was going to arrive at the coffee shop early and that I was welcome to join him. To be polite, I arrived about fifteen minutes before the "official" time of our date. When I went inside, I saw him sitting at a table with a drink in front of him. This time, I was mentally prepared for him to *not* buy me a drink—which was good because he didn't. He didn't even offer.

I learned my lesson last time, bro, I thought. *If you're not going to buy me a coffee, I'm not going to buy one at all. Apparently, you can afford a drink for yourself but not for me—and that's fine. Whatever.*

After James and I chatted for a few minutes, we started walking toward the area where the farmers market typically took place. I wasn't surprised that there were no booths, vendors, or customers in the area, but he was basically speechless. It took a while for him to realize his original plan had failed. I played dumb because I didn't want to make him feel bad. However, I *did* want to see him squirm a little. (He squirmed a lot.)

Instead of perusing produce and baked goods, we went on a walk. During our date, we discussed our allergies, our childhood pets, our homeschool experiences, and our plans for the remainder of the day. He said he was going to take a hike with his small group from church, and I said I was going to visit an amusement park with Anna. He *finally* asked about my hobbies. I'd been dying to tell him about them—especially writing—but I'd been waiting for him to ask. Unfortunately, we didn't stay on that topic very long.

After walking around the city for nearly an hour, James and I headed back to the coffee shop. We went inside and talked for a little while. An alarm on his phone went off at 9:30 a.m., reminding him to proceed to his next activity. That made me feel super loved.

In some ways, date #2 was better than date #1. James was less distracted. He actually seemed to enjoy our time together. He hugged me when I arrived *and* when I left.

Still, I felt frustrated with him. We made very little progress in our conversation—largely because he didn't steer it in any meaningful direction (again). He didn't ask many questions (again). He didn't offer to buy a coffee for me (again).

But he later texted to apologize for the change in plans that morning, thank me for my flexibility, and ask about my visit to the amusement park. He even asked if I'd convinced Anna to join me on any rides (which I appreciated because I'd brought up her aversion to rollercoasters during our date). Suddenly, I forgot why I was mad at him. So I asked about his hike, and he sent me a picture of him and his small group friends in front of a waterfall. Then I waited for him to ask me out on a third date. But setting it up proved to be a major challenge for him.

A couple days later, he asked if the upcoming weekend was the weekend I'd be out of town visiting my friend from college—a visit I'd mentioned on our date—so I told him the specific day and time I expected to be out of town. But instead of asking me to meet on a day and/or time *outside* the six hours I'd be away, he played hard-to-get: "Gotcha. I was looking ahead on my calendar to see if you wanted to meet up again at some point, but my next two weekends I'll be out of town."

I should've simply said, "Oh, that's nifty"—or perhaps nothing at all—but I responded rather eagerly: "Yeah, I'd like to see you again soon."

In his weak reply, he said, "[There's] a chance I could meet you somewhere Friday during the morning or around lunch. It would be play-by-ear though—I'm not sure how much work I'll have to get done that day before I head out for the weekend."

Ten minutes later, he sent an equally weak follow-up text: "That's also assuming you're not working at that time—which, if you are, then no worries; we can just find another time in the coming weeks."

But I didn't want to "find another time in the coming weeks." That was way too open-ended for me. I wanted to see him—like in the very near future. Perhaps even more than that, I wanted the relationship to *not* fizzle out. Frankly, I was afraid that if we didn't get a third date on the calendar *soon*, there wouldn't be a third date *ever*.

So I drove to the hoop: "I'll probably be working until 10 or 11 on Friday [morning], so if you're up for meeting, I'm down!"

"Okay, maybe something around lunch then," he said. "I'll have a better idea of if I can meet up or not . . . on Thursday evening, but in the meantime, is there anything in particular you'd maybe like to do?"

I was very tempted to tell him, "Actually, there *is* something I'd like to do. I'd like to let *you* pick what we do. Also, I'd like to *not* feel like an inconvenience to you. I thought you were into me, but if you're not, this is the time to say so. This playing-hard-to-get thing isn't cute or charming; it's annoying."

Of course, I didn't say that to him. Instead, I suggested going to lunch at a particular restaurant I liked, but I also mentioned taking a walk if he preferred that (since he seemed so averse to paying for things—specifically things for *me*). He said he loved the restaurant idea, suggested we meet at noon, and promised to let me know if anything needed to change.

Two days later, something did indeed need to change. He asked if we could move our lunch to a half hour earlier. I wanted to ask why he was treating our date like a doctor's appointment, but I simply said yes.

Though I was relieved to *finally* have the details for date #3 nailed down, I was also apprehensive about it. There were important things I needed to know about James, and I realized he probably wasn't going to share them with me unless I asked about them directly. *He* certainly wasn't in a hurry to find out anything important about *me*. So I mentally prepared myself to ask him some hard questions.

When we met for lunch on Friday, our conversation started off slow and casual—as it had for our first two dates—but once we ordered, I looked at him and awkwardly blurted out, "So I'm going to grill you now." The look on his face told me he wasn't ready to be grilled. Though I felt uncomfortable at first, it didn't take long for my questions to start flowing. The five specific things I asked about were his testimony, his walk with God, his views on alcohol, his political party, and his previous romantic relationships.

First, I asked how he became a Christian. His answer was vague at best. I also asked about his walk with God, hoping his response would include something about reading the Bible and praying on a daily basis, but his response was pretty hard to follow. I knew he was active in his church, and I liked that about him. But the fact that he couldn't articulate his own testimony—and the fact that he didn't ask about mine—concerned me.

Then I asked about his thoughts on alcohol. While we ultimately had the same take on it, the basis for his conclusion was very different from mine. I found it interesting that he asked if the alcohol thing was a "big deal" to me. I wanted to say, "Well, duh—I'm asking about it on our third date." However, I responded coolly and moved on to my next question.

I asked which candidate he voted for in the last presidential election, and he asked the same thing. The way he answered this question was similar to the way he'd answered my prior question. We voted for the same candidate but for totally different reasons.

Last, I broached the topic of his previous romantic relationships. Honestly, I wanted to ask if he was a virgin, but I didn't know how to ask that in a non-awkward way (probably because there's *not* a non-awkward way to ask such a question). While I was trying to get the words out, he said, "So . . . my dating history?" I rolled with it, and he proceeded to tell me about his ex-girlfriend—the "serious girlfriend" he'd mentioned on date #1—plus some other girls he'd dated. When he asked about my dating history, all I could say was that I'd liked a guy throughout college who had never liked me back. I hated how pathetic it sounded, but it was the truth. Until James entered my life, I didn't have a dating history.

Then James asked a couple questions of his own. First, he asked what I wanted my future to look like. I discussed my desires to write, get married, and have a family. In turn, I asked what he wanted his future to look like, and he talked about some of his interests. I already knew about his profession, and I admired that he worked hard. But frankly, I didn't share his deep passion for his specific career field.

Second, James asked about my thoughts on the singles' group, which we were in together. The mixer had been the launch event for the group, but since then, a board game party and a volleyball game had been organized. I liked the group, and I told him that. When I asked him the same thing, he expressed how much he liked it too. Then he said something totally unexpected.

"I become more fond of you each time we meet up."

The statement seemed to come out of nowhere. It was the first sweet thing he—or *any* guy—had ever said to me, so I had no clue how to respond. My body froze, but my heart began to melt.

Until it shattered.

Instead of following up the fond-of-you comment with something like, "I want to take you on a real date—like pick you up and buy you dinner at a nice restaurant," he took our conversation (and our relationship) in an unexpected direction.

"I'm taking a casual approach to this," he said in the next breath—with "casual" meaning "noncommittal" and "this" meaning "us."

Oh, I thought, feeling completely dumbfounded by what he said yet perfectly certain what he meant. *You're not interested in pursuing me; you're just "trying me out." I suppose you're going to move on to other girls in the singles' group because you prefer a girl who fawns over you—a girl who's too enraptured by your awesomeness to ask hard questions and speak her mind. Got it.*

He then added, "I'm not sure if I'm going to sign up for the walk-and-talk." He was referring to an upcoming event for the singles' group. I took the opportunity to tell him I'd already signed up for it. If he wanted me to know he was keeping his options open, I wanted him to know I was keeping my options open too. So I tried to act cool and imitate his nonchalance.

Frankly, there wasn't much left to say after that, so we wrapped up our conversation. I didn't realize that it would be our *last* conversation. I was in for a rude awakening.

Single Girl, my experience with James taught me lots of hard lessons, which I'll share with you throughout the next couple chapters. But the first hard lesson I want to share is this: Mutual interest isn't a sufficient foundation for marrying or even starting to date someone. If you notice a guy's yellow flags early on and decide to steer clear of him, you can avoid a great deal of heartache.

//

My son, give attention to my words;

Incline your ear to my sayings.

Do not let them depart from your sight;

Keep them in the midst of your heart.

For they are life to those who find them

And health to all their body.

> Watch over your heart with all diligence,
> For from it flow the springs of life.
> Put away from you a deceitful mouth
> And put devious speech far from you.
> Let your eyes look directly ahead
> And let your gaze be fixed straight in front of you.
> Watch the path of your feet
> And all your ways will be established.
> Do not turn to the right nor to the left;
> Turn your foot from evil.
> (Prov. 4:20-27 NASB)

Though I didn't spot James' red flags until after our relationship ended, I did spot some yellow flags while we were dating, and most of them fit into one of these broad categories: lack of compatibility, lack of commitment, and lack of character.

First, James and I lacked compatibility. We had major differences, even in our hobbies and interests. He liked running, hiking, and paddleboarding—all of which I dislike. He also enjoyed making crafts using rocks and shells. (No, I'm not kidding.) On date #2, he talked about his recent trip to a rock auction and his shell collection (which sounded disturbingly large). He was a chiropractor for women, children, and babies; I'd never gone to a chiropractor. His church belonged to a different denomination than mine. He was in a book club, and I hate reading books—plus, he was reading a book by a controversial author with whom I strongly disagree. On date #3, he told me that he was going on a trip to a mule festival with his roommate after our date. In addition to featuring a 5K walk/run, the mule festival showcased a "queen mule." (No, I'm not kidding about this either.) All I could do was smile and nod as I listened to him describe the event.

In a more general way, he and I were very different people. I'm a down-to-earth person. I'm willing to be open and honest with others, and I'm appreciative when they're willing to be open and honest with me. But he wasn't that kind of person. He was conceited and tried to impress others.

Honestly, I couldn't relate to much of what he said *or* how he said it. As a writer and speaker, I try very hard to communicate clearly. He, however, didn't communicate clearly at all. I had serious trouble following his train of thought at times. That actually makes sense now though. I've heard that—in general—people who aren't clear communicators aren't clear thinkers. I wanted him to simply say things with confidence and precision rather than mumbling or going down rabbit trails.

In short, we didn't vibe. But on a deeper level, our views on fundamental issues didn't align. We were far too different. I'm not saying two people with different passions and perspectives are destined for a failed relationship, but that *is* a legitimate possibility. My relationship with James sure didn't succeed.

Second, James lacked commitment. To be honest, I struggled to determine whether he truly liked me or not. Some things suggested that he did. He asked for my number. He asked me out three times. He told me he liked me.

But other things suggested that he didn't like me much at all. He didn't really flirt with me, compliment me, or attempt to woo me. He didn't pay for me on our first or second dates. I seriously wondered if a third date would happen because he *really* struggled to man up and ask me. He quickly followed up his statement about liking me with a statement that contradicted it.

I felt like he was sending me mixed messages. At times, I tried to justify his behavior and told myself stupid things like these: *He probably got burned in a previous relationship and doesn't want to rush into anything, so I just need to give him time. Plus, he's a real person, not an actor in a Hallmark movie, so I shouldn't expect him to be absolutely crazy about me.*

Frankly, however, he wasn't that into me. Though that statement is painful to write, it's true. He wasn't committed to me or our relationship. I wanted him to be all-in, but he just wasn't.

Third, James lacked character. When our relationship started, his lack of character was a pale yellow flag. (When our relationship ended, it was a bright red flag—but I'll share more about that in chapter 8.) Though he was a little too competitive, I tried to cut him some slack because I knew competitiveness was common for guys. Overall, he seemed nice.

I did have serious concerns about his faith. Honestly, his inability to articulate how he *became* a Christian made me wonder if he actually *was* a Christian. I didn't know his heart, but I knew his testimony was fuzzy. Similarly, while I appreciated that he attended and served at church, I had trouble understanding what his relationship with God looked like beyond church involvement.

His ambivalence to my own relationship with God bothered me too. I brought up the faith thing on our third date, so he didn't even have to come up with the "right" questions to ask me. All he had to do was return my questions—but he didn't.

He *did* want to know how I stayed active though. We talked about it on our first date. He was interested in my workout routine but uninterested in my testimony, which was odd to me. But I suppose it ultimately pointed to poorly ordered priorities. Health (at least, *his* definition of it) was the only thing he took a strong stance on. He was genuinely obsessed with it. It seemed to ultimately determine his views on important subjects like alcohol and politics. As a former anorexic, all I could see were the potential dangers of his obsession. I didn't understand why he grounded his beliefs in health—something that's subjective and ever-changing—instead of the infallible Word of God. Health mattered more to him than perhaps anything else.

After my third date with James, I felt torn at first, unsure whether his yellow flags were deal-breakers or not. However, it didn't take long for me to realize they were. When I told my family what James had said and gave it more thought, I became certain the relationship needed to end—but I never got the chance to do it.

Even though I didn't see his *red* flags until after our relationship ended, his *yellow* flags showed me all I needed to know: He wasn't the right guy for me. I want to marry a man who makes me smile and laugh (not contort my face), loves me deeply (not half-heartedly), and puts Christ first in his life (not second). I don't expect him to be perfect, but I do expect to see more green flags—and fewer yellow ones.

Single Girl, if you like a certain guy but see a lack of compatibility, a lack of commitment, and/or a lack of character, he's probably not the right guy for you—and it's probably time to move on because he's just holding you up from meeting the right guy. Yellow flags often indicate that a relationship should end (or not even start). Like red flags, yellow flags don't magically disappear once a relationship reaches a specific point. Honestly, they sometimes become worse—or even multiply—as time goes on. If a guy isn't the right guy *now*, it's unlikely he'll somehow *become* the right guy as your boyfriend, fiancé, or husband.

The book of Proverbs says, "The simple believes everything, but the prudent gives thought to his steps. One who is wise is cautious and turns away from evil, but a fool is reckless and careless" (Prov. 14:15-16 ESV). Yellow flags might seem trivial, but there are significant consequences for ignoring them. Although forcing a fit in a relationship can lead to resentment and regret, letting go of the wrong guy can lead to God's blessings.

Don't believe everything you hear from the guy you like or assume his faults will vanish over time. Instead, observe what decisions he makes and why he makes them. Pay attention to what his weaknesses are and how he addresses them. Consider how your future with him could look. Letting your guard down is one of the worst relationship mistakes you can make.

In short, don't just look the other way when you see yellow flags. They merit thoughtful consideration, fervent prayer, and godly counsel. My desire is to spare you from the pain that lies beyond them.

Maddie's Story

When I walked into the restaurant, I knew the question I needed to ask my date—but I was incredibly nervous about asking it.

I met this guy through a dating app. I quickly learned he was a Christian, but as we talked during our first date, I noticed he didn't really discuss his faith—besides mentioning the church he attended. I knew I needed to ask what his relationship with God looked like on a daily basis, but I felt anxious because I realized I might not hear the answer I *wanted* to hear.

I recognized the importance of only dating guys who had active relationships with God, but I *so* wanted my relationship to work out. I was tempted to focus on what his character qualities were or how much fun we had together. But deep down, I knew that if he wasn't growing in his faith, our relationship couldn't ultimately be what God had in store for me.

All that to say, I understand the desire to settle—to accept the "good enough" guy. I've been there. I've hoped and prayed for him to be enough. But what our Heavenly Father has planned for us in the future is so much better than the relationships we could settle for now.

If you desire to marry a guy who lives out his faith, keep waiting. The Lord is patient and kind. Though this season of singleness can feel long and frustrating, He's ultimately working for your good and His glory (Rom. 8:28). Everything will be worth the wait.

~Maddie, Single Girl~

Chapter 8

Grieving the End of a Relationship ~~Does~~ Doesn't Mean I'm Weak

Dear Single Girl,

Not long ago, I got my first broken heart, thanks to James. Frankly, the way he rejected me hurt more than the rejection itself. Rather than being upfront with me, he abruptly ghosted me and almost immediately jumped into a relationship with another girl. I saw him multiple times after our final date, but he intentionally ignored me. He never explained why he decided to reject me, but deep down, I knew the reason: He was insecure, immature, and intimidated.

Honestly, there are no stages for my post-James grief; there are only deep, painful emotions that seem permanently present in my life. Perhaps these emotions will disappear soon. I certainly hope they will. But I tend to believe they'll accompany me for a while longer.

I didn't expect my first relationship to turn out this way. Nor did I expect to have such an intense emotional response to its end. Until James broke my heart, I thought I was a strong person. However, this experience has shown me how fragile I really am.

Single Girl, I understand that losing a relationship can be incredibly painful, even if that's ultimately the best thing for it. Maybe the guy had a mean streak, a dangerous addiction, or a checkered past. There's a reason—or perhaps many reasons—you're no longer with him.

Yet something inside you misses him. You wish he were still in your life. No matter how hard you try to stop thinking about him, you keep failing. He moved on long ago, but you're right where he left you.

Although you might *feel* helpless to get past your grief, you *can* get past it. It's simply going to require some time (and faith). Ultimately, the emotional healing process is in God's hands, just like everything else in your life. This process probably won't be *easy*, but if you allow Him to carry you through it, you'll see it's *possible*.

Love, Grace

Even though I knew date #3 didn't go super well, I still hoped James would ask me out again so I could turn him down. Honestly, I agonized over the situation. I waited impatiently for him to reach out, begging God to make him text me and constantly checking my phone to see if he had. At the very least, I thought he'd tell me, "It's been fun getting to know you, but I don't think we should move forward" or "You're a great person, but I don't feel like we're a great fit." I *definitely* didn't expect him to ghost me, but that's *exactly* what he did.

On the surface, maybe James didn't feel the need to end the relationship in a clear, direct way (though I would've greatly appreciated that). But maybe—beyond simply trying to avoid an unfun conversation—he was insecure, immature, and intimidated. Those three traits seemed to define him, and unfortunately, they defined his approach to our relationship.

I think he could detect my dissatisfaction with the way he answered my questions on our third date. I didn't flat-out tell him I disliked what he said or how he said it. But I'm sure he wanted me to agree with him on everything—and perhaps even remark on how insightful his views were—and I'm sure he noticed I didn't. Plus, my natural tendency is to wear my feelings on my face when I interact with people, and my face probably told him I wasn't his biggest fan.

I also think he could detect that I played hard-to-get. From the moment we met to the moment we parted ways, I tried to avoid looking or sounding desperate for him. I certainly enjoyed his attention and flirted with him at times, but I didn't throw myself at him. I wanted him to lead the relationship, so I let him pursue me—until he decided he didn't want to pursue me anymore. Apparently, he wasn't ready to lead the relationship. Perhaps the chase was more challenging than he expected.

I now wonder if the questions he asked and the comments he made on our third date were him giving me opportunities to say I was into him. When he asked what I thought about the singles' group, maybe he wanted me to say, "It's been great—after all, I met *you* through it." When he told me he was taking a casual approach, maybe he wanted me to say, "But I really like you, so I want to take a *serious* approach." When he mentioned he was unsure about signing up for the walk-and-talk, maybe he wanted me to say, "Well, I'm not going to sign up for it because *you're* my person now."

But since I was determined not to be desperate, I decided that if he wanted me to say I was into him, he'd have to say he was into me first—and "I become more fond of you each time we meet up" didn't count as an admission of his affection since he immediately followed it up with, "I'm taking a casual approach to this."

Even though James clearly wasn't the right guy for me, being ghosted by him was still hard. I felt vulnerable because the situation was entirely out of my control. I felt disgusted because he never even tried to ask me out a fourth time despite claiming to like me. I felt hurt because he essentially rejected me.

My first post-James cry happened three days after our third date. I was genuinely surprised he hadn't reached out to me—not even to say he wasn't interested in moving forward. But beyond surprise, I felt a deep sense of helplessness.

He didn't end the relationship. *I* didn't end the relationship. The relationship just *ended.*

Hence why I cried in the middle of a work meeting on a Monday afternoon. (Thankfully, it was a virtual meeting, and my camera and microphone were off.) I started weeping quietly while sitting alone at my desk at home. I simply couldn't hold back the tears any longer.

My pain intensified when I saw James at a volleyball game for the singles' group six days later and he ignored me. He acted like nothing had happened between us. Like he hadn't met me, asked me out, or dated me. Like he hadn't told me he was fond of me. Like he hadn't ghosted me. I knew him better than any other guy on the court, and he knew me better than any other girl on the court. Yet he gave me the cold shoulder, treating me like a complete stranger.

To make the situation worse, Holly—a girl in the singles' group who looked eerily similar to me—adored James. She wanted him *bad*. Watching them flirt at that volleyball game was painful. I wanted to cry afterward, but the tears didn't come until the following day—during *another* virtual meeting for work.

Four days later, I went to another volleyball game for the singles' group. When I arrived, James wasn't there—but he showed up later (of course). Jealousy overcame me as I watched him and Holly flirt. I was on his team twice in a row, but he still managed to avoid me.

"James couldn't take the heat," Jenna told me on the drive home that night. "He knew you were going to reject him, so he ran away with his tail between his legs."

Even though I genuinely appreciated the sentiment, I still felt very upset about the situation. The next day, I was off work for a holiday, and I spent much of my time working on this book—specifically this chapter about losing James. Tears threatened to brim over as I typed, but I held them back as long as I could. Finally, I went to my room, laid on my bed, and cried.

Then it happened again—for the third Monday afternoon in a row, I started crying during my virtual work meeting simply because I felt sad about the situation.

Three days later, I cried while I was writing a report for work and listening to a song about God's unchanging nature. I'd wanted to cry all day, but the song lyrics triggered my tears because they reminded me of God's steadiness—and my unsteadiness. I hated feeling like an emotional wreck.

Why can't I just get over this jerk? I thought. *When will I stop thinking about him and crying about him? When will I start feeling normal again?*

Unfortunately, the situation got worse instead of better.

The infamous walk-and-talk took place a couple days later. Even though James had expressed uncertainty about signing up for it, I thought he'd end up coming. I actually *hoped* he'd end up coming because I wanted him to be forced to talk to me and clear the air and apologize. Deep down, I also wanted to spend time with him because I missed him.

But James didn't come. Neither did Holly. Both of them had been active members of the singles' group, which made me wonder if they were no longer "on the market."

Reality smacked me in the face during a volleyball game for the singles' group three days later. I actually thought I was doing okay. I hadn't cried in five days, which was a new record for me in my post-James era. Holly tried to make small talk with me at the event, which was extremely awkward. I didn't see James—until about half an hour into the night.

James hugged Holly when he arrived. Instead of playing volleyball with everyone else, they sat on the sidelines to flirt. They couldn't take their eyes off each other. With every move he made, it felt like he was twisting a knife in my heart—the same knife he'd stabbed in it three and a half weeks earlier.

Ugh! I wanted to scream. *Why are you here? This is an event for* singles, *and you two are clearly* together. *Please go somewhere—anywhere—so I don't have to watch this any longer.*

I tried to maintain my composure, but I thought I was going to lose it right there on the court.

"Can we *please* leave?" I hissed at my sisters, who were at the event with me. They made me stay for another game. Though I was livid about it in the moment, I'm now thankful they made me stay, simply to show James he couldn't get to me.

But after that game, I insisted we leave because I truly couldn't bear to look at James and Holly for another second. Of course, they left the volleyball court (*together*) at the same time we left, but there was no turning back at that point. As soon as I got in the car, I had a meltdown.

Since my sisters and I had made plans earlier in the day to go to Cracker Barrel after the game, that's where we headed. But I cried on the way to the restaurant, in the restaurant, and on the way home from the restaurant. The sadness, anger, bitterness, and frustration hit me so hard I couldn't help but cry. I felt like I was at rock bottom.

Seriously, what's wrong with me? I thought. *He's moved on, but I'm right where he left me. He's forgotten about me, and all I can do is think about him. He's shown no remorse for how he's treated me, yet I keep crying about how much I miss him. I absolutely hate that I still like him.*

Thankfully, when I couldn't be patient with myself, the Lord was patient with me. He saw when I held back tears and when I let them fall. He heard my cries of despair. He felt my broken heart and my crushed spirit. But instead of turning away from me—like James had—He drew near.

Single Girl, your sadness, anger, bitterness, and frustration about a relationship ending are legitimate. It doesn't matter if the guy you were dating was incredible or terrible. It doesn't matter if the relationship lasted three weeks or three years. It doesn't matter if you ended it or he ended it or it simply ended. Keep seeking God in the midst of your grief. He'll heal your broken heart in due time.

//

I sought the LORD, and He answered me,
And delivered me from all my fears.
They looked to Him and were radiant,
And their faces will never be ashamed.
This poor man cried, and the LORD heard him
And saved him out of all his troubles.
The angel of the LORD encamps around those who fear Him,
And rescues them.

O taste and see that the LORD is good;
How blessed is the man who takes refuge in Him!
O fear the LORD, you His saints;
For to those who fear Him there is no want.
The young lions do lack and suffer hunger;
But they who seek the LORD shall not be in want of any good thing.
Come, you children, listen to me;
I will teach you the fear of the LORD.
Who is the man who desires life
And loves length of days that he may see good?

Keep your tongue from evil
And your lips from speaking deceit.
Depart from evil and do good;
Seek peace and pursue it.

The eyes of the LORD are toward the righteous
And His ears are open to their cry.
The face of the LORD is against evildoers,
To cut off the memory of them from the earth.
The righteous cry, and the LORD hears
And delivers them out of all their troubles.
The LORD is near to the brokenhearted
And saves those who are crushed in spirit.
(Ps. 34:4-18 NASB)

In my pre-James era, I wasn't a big crier. Tears only came every now and then. However, that changed when our relationship ended. During a seven-week period, I cried seven times, which felt like seven times too many. But as I grieved, Psalm 34 brought me comfort. I actually started memorizing it.

Though I realize that bursting into tears isn't always the best way to deal with grief, I don't think God is intimidated by the number of meltdowns I have. After all, He catches every tear I cry (Ps. 56:8). I'm confident He can handle my grief. He doesn't ignore me when I'm in pain; He sees, hears, and comforts me. Ultimately, I can't heal my broken heart, but He can—and He will (Ps. 147:3).

When emotional moments come, I need to seek the Lord instead of believing things like these: "People go through breakups all the time—and this isn't even a breakup! You only went out with James a few times. Plus, he hasn't even treated you well. You're being a baby about this. Get it together!"

God's voice is so much gentler: "Grace, you're not a robot; you're a real person with real feelings. You've experienced something painful. The way James treated you isn't good or kind or right. But I'm near to you, and I'm in control of this situation. Give yourself grace to grieve."

I actually made a bookmark for my Bible with this verse on it: "This poor man cried, and the LORD heard him and saved him out of all his troubles" (Ps. 34:6 NASB). Honestly, I made it because I needed to remember *I'm* the poor man whom the Lord hears and saves. I don't have to pretend I'm fine when I'm not fine. He knows me. Deep down, I'm extremely fragile. But the emotional healing process isn't about my ability to effortlessly move on; it's about God's willingness to meet me in my grief and deliver me from it—one day at a time.

For the most part, the emotional healing process has been out of my control. I've had to allow God to heal my heart in His time and in His way. However, there are a couple action steps I've taken as I've grieved the end of the relationship.

The first was starting to pray daily for God to replace my sadness, anger, bitterness, and frustration with His peace because it surpasses all understanding (Phil. 4:7).

The second was starting to tell myself the truth daily. I felt like God whispered these words to me about James, so I wrote them down on a sticky note and placed it on my computer monitor for work: "I have someone better for you; just hold on and trust Me." I also made two lists about James—one list with sixteen reasons he wasn't the right guy for me and one list with four broad reminders about the situation. I taped both lists to my bathroom mirror and read them for sixty days straight. And I actually want to share the second list here.

First, I reminded myself that the situation wasn't really about Holly; it was about James.

On the night of my post-volleyball-game meltdown, I was pretty irritated with James *and* Holly. But mainly, I felt hurt by James. I just didn't understand why he came to the volleyball game even though he was clearly dating Holly. I didn't realize until later that he probably came in an effort to prove he didn't need me (or my convictions, confidence, and clarity—all of which apparently became painfully obvious to him on our third date). I also think he resented that I wasn't desperate for him (unlike Holly). Frankly, however, he failed to make the point I believe he came to make that night. In trying so hard to prove I meant nothing to him, he proved I *did* mean something to him. He also proved how insecure, immature, and intimidated he really was.

Second, I reminded myself that James had shown me his true colors—and that they weren't pretty.

Initially, James seemed like a nice guy. However, I quickly began to see things in him that I couldn't unsee and hear things from him that I couldn't unhear. The way he talked and acted on our third date was very revealing—and his true colors only became more obvious (and unattractive) as time passed. I couldn't ignore the way he treated me afterward. His decision to ghost me and then immediately pair off with another girl showed me everything I needed to know.

Third, I reminded myself that James would reap what he'd sown.

To be honest, it felt basically impossible to let go of my bitterness toward James. He hurt me deeply, and I wanted to hurt him deeply in return. But the author of Hebrews stated, "Pursue peace with all men, and the sanctification without which no one will see the Lord. See to it that no one comes short of the grace of God; that no root of bitterness springing up causes trouble, and by it many be defiled" (Heb. 12:14-15 NASB). I had to take my bitterness to God over and over again—and I still do. It was His job, not mine, to deal with James. I knew he'd reap the seeds of hostility he'd sown, and I knew I needed to sow seeds of kindness. As Paul wrote in his letter to the Galatians, "Do not be deceived, God is not mocked; for whatever a man sows, this he will also reap" (Gal. 6:7 NASB).

Fourth, I reminded myself that James wasn't a good guy and that being with him wasn't God's will for me.

Even on the hardest days of my post-James era, I didn't have to wonder if I'd come to the right conclusion about him. God's will is for husbands and wives to be one flesh—unified partners for life—and James and I could never have been one flesh. He lacked some essential character qualities and possessed some views that greatly differed from mine. Plus, he didn't hold all the convictions I held. Sure, I could've simply echoed his sentiments, pretending I wholeheartedly agreed with him on everything. If I had, we might still be together—but honestly, I'd have so much guilt because he wasn't the right guy for me. Even though I missed him, *not* being with him was God's will for me. I could have peace knowing I'd followed God and the convictions He'd given me.

Though my disappointment about losing James remains, God's presence remains too. I'm grateful for His constancy. My ups and downs don't change His character or promises because He's always and forever steady.

Single Girl, grieving the end of a relationship is perfectly normal. You don't need to pretend you're fine when you're not fine. Having emotions—including the unfun ones—is part of being human. Though it might take several weeks, months, or even years for your broken heart to heal, it *will* heal if you take your pain to the right place.

Remember the Lord is near. He's near when you see your ex-boyfriend flirting with another girl after your breakup. He's near when you look at photos of you and your ex-boyfriend having fun together. He's near when you hear your ex-boyfriend's voice in your head, saying he'll love you forever and never let you go.

Ultimately, you're not able to save yourself from post-breakup grief. But you're not completely helpless in the emotional healing process. Even when you're in pain, you can do exactly what Psalm 34 says: Seek the Lord, fix your eyes on Him, fear Him, notice His goodness, take refuge in Him, avoid saying malicious and deceitful things (especially about your ex-boyfriend), depart from evil, do good, pursue peace, and cry out to Him.

Grab a box of tissues and let your mascara run rather than bottling up your grief. I promise God can handle it. In fact, He *wants* to handle it—but you have to let Him.

Emily's Story

Over the last six months, I've done some things I'm proud of, as well as some things I'm ashamed of. These things have taught me that one of the most difficult parts of singleness is *not* having someone to share in my successes and failures. I've experienced both alone.

Earlier this year, I received a promotion that I hadn't expected to receive for several years. I was excited about it, but it was difficult to reach the end of the day and realize I had no one there to share in the excitement with me. I want someone who knows my deepest thoughts and biggest dreams to rejoice with me in my accomplishments. It feels selfish, but I want to be with someone who's ready to put the feather in my cap; I don't want to do it myself. I used to think my season of singleness would be a great time to focus on my career so I could slow down later when I started a family. This has been true to some extent, but I didn't foresee the loneliness this season would bring.

The other—and honestly much worse—side of this coin is that I have to bear the weight of my failures alone. When I'm angry, there's no one to listen to me. When I'm upset, I feel more alone than I ever thought possible because there's no one to tell me not to worry and assure me he's there for me. When I hurt other people, there's no one to correct me or encourage me to make things right. As I zoom in on all of my mistakes, I desperately wish I had someone in my life to pull the magnifying glass out of my hand and calm my fears. I crave the perspective a life partner can provide, but—at least for now—I have to be okay without that.

~Emily, Single Girl~

Chapter 9

My Dating ~~Is~~ Isn't Wasted

Dear Single Girl,

When I met a tall, dark, and handsome guy named James who got my number, asked me out, and told me he was fond of me, I got a taste of something beautifully brand-new—how it felt to be liked by a guy I liked. He was the first guy who chose me. Of all the girls he met at the mixer, he chose to pursue me, get to know me, and date me. I was so taken aback yet so ready.

However, James was also the first guy who rejected me. Without a single word of explanation, he abandoned me. It was honestly one of the hardest experiences I've ever had. I couldn't help but wonder why all of it—or *any* of it—had happened.

Single Girl, if you've ever wondered about the purpose of a relationship that no longer exists, you're in good company. A breakup involves lots of emotions, as I talked about in chapter 8. It usually involves lots of unanswered questions too.

When a relationship ends, you might be tempted to view it as pointless. After all, you genuinely thought it was going somewhere, and it went absolutely nowhere. You can't get back the time you invested in it—or the tears you've shed since it ended. But the relationship you wish you could erase from your life can't be erased. Trust me when I say that's good news. The Lord's perfect plan for you is unfolding, even if you can't fully understand it. He never makes mistakes or wastes experiences.

Love, Grace

//

As I grieved the end of my relationship with James, I simultaneously tried to make sense of the relationship's purpose. But frankly, the relationship didn't seem to *have* a purpose. The words we'd exchanged, the texts we'd sent, and the moments we'd shared all felt meaningless because they'd ultimately led to heartbreak.

Cynical questions like these filled my mind: *What was the point of all this? What was the point of me meeting James, getting to know him, and falling for him? What was the point of him being interested in me, asking for my number, and asking me out?*

I wondered if the point of the whole experience was to scare me away from dating. If so, it worked. I couldn't go through that again. I felt worse off *after* meeting James than *before* meeting him. At one point in my grief, I wrote this in my journal: "GOD, WHY DID YOU MAKE ALL THIS HAPPEN TO ME?"

At times, I wished that it hadn't happened—that I hadn't gone out with James or given him my number or even met him. Though unrequited love wasn't fun or easy, I was used to it. I *wasn't* used to being chosen, then rejected, then replaced.

But it *had* happened—and I desperately desired to know why. I wanted to understand why God had allowed us to meet . . . and fall for each other . . . and start dating. I also wanted to understand why God had allowed James to break my heart. He could've kept us apart, but instead, He'd brought us together. It didn't make sense to me.

To be honest, I still don't know why I had the experience. But I do know it wasn't wasted. The series of events that ultimately led me to a relationship with James demonstrates God's providence far too clearly for the experience to have been a mistake.

This series of events began when a girl named Kendra decided to start a singles' group in my area. She was tired of using dating apps, and she wanted to make real connections with real people—and provide opportunities for other Christian singles to do the same. The first activity she organized was a mixer at a coffee shop. She posted about it on social media and put up flyers for it at local businesses.

When Jillian—a mom in my young adult group at church—saw one of the flyers, she took a picture of it and sent the picture in the group chat for my young adult group. A couple friends then texted me and my sisters, encouraging us to sign up. Even though we'd never gone to a singles' mixer, we decided to try it.

Two weeks later, on the morning of the mixer, I wrote this prayer in my journal: "Dear God, please help the singles' mixer go well today. I have a strange combination of feelings—fear, excitement, and nervousness. . . . I know You're so much more than a vending machine. . . . But I know only You can make something—anything—happen at the event today. You control and are sovereign over everything. You uphold the entire universe with Your word. I trust

You and love You no matter what happens today. But I'm asking for You to move—to connect me and my sisters with three godly guys. That's my request."

When I wrote that prayer, no one had ever asked me out. In fact, five days before that, I'd published a blog post entitled "1 Thing Every Inexperienced Dater Needs to Know." I'd opened up about feeling like an outsider due to my lack of dating experience. But I'd also shared Jeremiah 17:5-8 and talked about trusting the Lord during seemingly barren seasons—specifically singleness.

I couldn't have predicted that five days after publishing that post, I'd meet a guy who would actually take me on my first date and make me a (more) experienced dater. It didn't happen during my four years attending a Christian college or during my four years trying young adult groups at endless churches. It happened at a "random" mixer. All of a sudden, my seemingly barren season didn't feel so barren anymore.

I won't repeat the details of how I met James since I shared them in chapter 7, but we definitely hit it off at the mixer—me with him *and* him with me, which was a first. And two of James' friends, Cole and Wes, hit it off with my sisters. Through a hilarious mingle bingo-related miscommunication, Cole ended up with Anna's number.

Though I was happy about meeting James at the mixer, I honestly didn't know if I'd ever see him again. We didn't attend the same church, and we weren't in the same friend group. We didn't even live in the same city technically. Worst of all, we didn't have a way to communicate because he hadn't gotten my number.

With anticipation—and apprehension—I wrote this prayer in my journal the day after the mixer: "Dear God . . . I really like James. He was attentive and interesting and sweet and cute. He has a real job. . . . He could have a normal conversation. He [could] make eye contact. He was homeschooled. He's from the North but loves . . . the South. I pray now that You'll lead us back to [each other] somehow. Please let us be able to see each other again soon. I'd really like to talk to him more. And I'd really like him to ask me out. Please, Lord—make this happen." I also thanked God for answering my prayer the previous day by connecting me and my sisters with guys at the mixer.

On the days that followed, I lifted up similar prayers about James. He wasn't the first guy I'd liked or prayed about. I'd crushed on countless guys in the past—including many who are mentioned in this book—but it clearly hadn't been God's will for me to date them because none of them had asked me out. In one prayer I wrote after the mixer, I actually told God about my fear that the situation with James would turn out like the situation with Sean—i.e., that I'd be interested in him but he wouldn't be interested in me.

But God would soon make it obvious that unlike Sean, James *was* interested in me; it would simply take a unique scenario—a right-place-at-the-right-time kind of scenario—for him to work up the nerve to do something about it.

As I was worrying about James, Anna was going out with Cole from the mixer. After their first date, he invited her to play pickleball with him and his friends at an indoor court on an upcoming Saturday morning. She asked if she could bring me and Jenna along, and he said yes. We later found out Wes would be there. When Saturday morning arrived, I prayed James would be there too. And he was.

Honestly, the outing felt like a triple date. Anna was on a team with Cole, Jenna was on a team with Wes, and I was on a team with James. We played pickleball for nearly two hours, though there were some opportunities to take breaks in between games. While we were there,

Wes asked for Jenna's number and asked her out. James and I chatted a little, but he didn't make any bold moves.

When our time slot at the indoor court ended, we went to a local restaurant for lunch. As we talked about various topics, we discovered we *all* had attended the *same* worship concert literally a *week* before the mixer. Cole, Wes, and James had sat just a couple rows behind me and my sisters.

Though James didn't say much at lunch, I figured he was probably socially exhausted. But apparently, the morning had bolstered his courage because as I stood up to leave the restaurant, he blurted out, "Grace! Would you mind if I got your number?" He murmured something about adding me to an adventure group chat, but I never got added to it (which was a relief because I'm not a big fan of adventures). Instead, I got a text from him that night. He said he'd enjoyed hanging out with me and my sisters and asked if I was interested in getting coffee with him.

I covered the rest of the story in chapters 7 and 8, but here, I want to focus on God's providence in the details.

If Kendra hadn't started the singles' group, she wouldn't have organized the mixer. If Kendra hadn't organized the mixer, Jillian wouldn't have shared the flyer for it. If Jillian hadn't shared the flyer for the mixer, Anna wouldn't have met Cole. If Anna hadn't met Cole, she wouldn't have accidentally given him her number. If Anna hadn't accidentally given Cole her number, he wouldn't have asked her out. If Cole hadn't asked Anna out, he wouldn't have invited her to play pickleball with him and his friends. If Cole hadn't invited Anna to play pickleball with him and his friends, I wouldn't have gotten to spend one-on-one time with James. If I hadn't gotten to spend one-on-one time with James, he wouldn't have asked for my number. If James hadn't asked for my number, I wouldn't have gone out with him.

Anna's relationship with Cole actually ended four days after the pickleball outing. (When they went out again, she realized he wasn't the right guy for her.) But if Cole hadn't set up the outing, let me and Jenna join, and brought James along, it's likely that James never would've felt comfortable enough to ask me out. As I mentioned in chapter 8, I eventually discovered he was insecure, immature, and intimidated at his core. James asking for my number and asking me out once—let alone three times—was clearly a God thing because he was so skittish. Nothing in him could've spurred him to take such bold steps; God was at work in each one.

For my first relationship to happen, a hundred stars had to align. Ultimately, that's why I know that *nothing* about the experience was a waste. I believe God aligned each of those stars to remind me that He can lead me to an unexpected person in an unexpected place at an unexpected time.

Yes, the "why" of my relationship with James is still a mystery to me, but God's providence in it isn't. He orchestrated its start and its end—and every moment in between. I hadn't developed even a *semblance* of a relationship with any other guy at any other point in my life. God intentionally placed James in my life and me in James' life. Our relationship wasn't an accident; it was God's plan for me all along.

Single Girl, I don't want you to spend another moment wondering if your relationships have been wasted. *They haven't been.* Even if you don't know the "why" of each dating experience, you can trust that each one matters. What might feel like a fluke—or even a failure—is a purposeful part of God's plan for you.

//

The plans of the heart belong to man,
But the answer of the tongue is from the LORD.
All the ways of a man are clean in his own sight,
But the LORD weighs the motives.
Commit your works to the LORD
And your plans will be established.
The LORD has made everything for its own purpose,
Even the wicked for the day of evil.
Everyone who is proud in heart is an abomination to the LORD;
Assuredly, he will not be unpunished.
By lovingkindness and truth iniquity is atoned for,
And by the fear of the LORD one keeps away from evil.
When a man's ways are pleasing to the LORD,
He makes even his enemies to be at peace with him.
Better is a little with righteousness
Than great income with injustice.
The mind of man plans his way,
But the LORD directs his steps.
(Prov. 16:1-9 NASB)

When I was a senior in high school, Proverbs 16:9 was my favorite verse. During that season of my life, I was extremely worried about the future. Still, I knew that no matter what field I studied in college or what career I found afterward, God's perfect plan would prevail.

Though several years have passed since then, the truth in that verse remains the same. God is sovereign over my plans, experiences, and outcomes. He knows the before, during, and after, and they're all under His control. If He's truly "made everything for its own purpose"—as Proverbs 16:4 (NASB) says—I don't have to wonder if my relationship with James happened for a reason.

That passage from Proverbs is similar to this passage from Psalms: "The steps of a man are established by the LORD, and He delights in his way. When he falls, he will not be hurled headlong, because the LORD is the One who holds his hand" (Ps. 37:23-24 NASB). I've had to keep in mind that my steps to James were ordained by God. He established my steps that led me to the mixer where I crossed paths with him, the pickleball outing where he gained the courage to ask for my number, the coffee shop where we met for our first date, the streets where we walked during our second date, and the café where we ate on our third date.

Yes, I *felt* like I was being hurled headlong when my relationship with James ended—especially because it ended in such an abrupt, painful way. But God was holding my hand the entire time. Though He didn't delight in my sorrow, He did delight in the unfolding of His perfect plan for me, which is rooted in His perfect love.

To be honest, the experience did shake my faith and leave me questioning why God had allowed me to go through it. Sometimes, I had to intentionally remind myself of the truth—like by writing this verse on a bookmark for my journal: "casting all your anxiety on Him, because He cares for you" (1 Pet. 5:7 NASB). Other times, God used specific things and people to remind me of the truth.

One person the Lord used was my friend Lucy. I'd met her at a writers' conference in early 2024. I hadn't seen her since then, and we hadn't texted much. But less than an hour after I published my first blog post about James—a post that had been emotionally draining to write—Lucy sent me this text: "Nothing is wasted, and I'm so thankful you know that the Creator God who designed your delightful soul would not have you settle for a man who can't treasure it. The Lord knows the desires of your heart, and He will answer your longing in due time and in His way, which is the way of love. May He comfort you, strengthen you, and give you laughter. Amen."

The words "nothing is wasted" stopped me in my tracks. I'd been desperately needing to hear them for weeks. Lucy's text reminded me that God had someone far better for me than James. It also reminded me that I didn't need to know the "why" of my experience with him because God knew it.

After yet another difficult volleyball game for the singles' group—one where I noticed James and Holly arriving together, heard them flirting, and saw them holding hands—I really felt like God was rubbing the James-and-Holly thing in my face. The next morning, I wrote an angry prayer about the experience. But when I started my workday afterward, I saw a message from my coworker essentially telling me that James wasn't the right guy but that the right guy would come.

Like Lucy's message, my coworker's message offered the specific encouragement I needed, in the specific moment I needed it. Through my coworker, God reminded me, "Grace, I see your pain, and I hear your prayers. I'm going to sustain you through this. Don't turn away from Me. Keep bringing your pain and your prayers to Me. Continue seeking Me."

There was also a sermon series at my church that seemed to have providential timing. It was about the life of Joseph, and it was ending as my relationship with James was ending. Though I knew Joseph's suffering far exceeded mine, I could relate to his story. What he said to his brothers when they came to him for food during a worldwide famine was particularly striking:

> "And now do not be distressed or angry with yourselves because you sold me here, for God sent me before you to preserve life. For the famine has been in the land these two years, and there are yet five years in which there will be neither plowing nor harvest. And God sent me before you to preserve for you a remnant on earth, and to keep alive for you many survivors. So it was not you who sent me here, but God. He has made me a father to Pharaoh, and lord of all his house and ruler over all the land of Egypt." (Gen. 45:5-8 ESV)

After their father died, the brothers feared Joseph would take revenge on them for treating him so terribly in the past (Gen. 50:15). But instead of scorning them, Joseph echoed his prior sentiments:

> So they sent a message to Joseph, saying, "Your father gave this command before he died: 'Say to Joseph, "Please forgive the transgression of your brothers and their sin, because they did evil to you."' And now, please forgive the transgression of the servants of the God of your father." Joseph wept when they spoke to him. His brothers also came and fell down before him and said, "Behold, we are your servants." But Joseph said to them, "Do not fear, for am I in the place of God? As for you, you meant evil against me, but God meant it for good, to bring it about that many people should be kept alive, as they are today. So do not fear; I will provide for you and your little ones." Thus he comforted them and spoke kindly to them. (Gen. 50:16-21 ESV)

Joseph's perspective on suffering is comforting, and his treatment toward his brothers is convicting. Ultimately, I believe Joseph was able to choose forgiveness over revenge because he understood that God had been at work throughout his life, even in the pain his brothers had inflicted on him. It wasn't wasted. In fact, it was used by God "that many people [would] be kept alive" (Gen. 50:20 ESV).

Though James might've intended to harm me, God intended good things to come from the relationship. I can't see every good thing He has done, is doing, or will do through it. But I can definitely see a couple of them.

One good thing I've seen God do through my experience with James is spur me to take my worries to Him and commit rich truths about His love to memory. Since the day I met James, I've mentioned him in more than fifty of my journaled prayers. Plus, I specifically lifted up prayers for wisdom about him many times, which God answered by making it very clear very quickly that he wasn't the right guy for me. And the end of my relationship with James was actually an answer to the prayers I've prayed for years about my future husband—including my specific requests for God to help us not settle for the wrong people and for Him to lead us to each other at the right time, in the right way. By helping me not settle for James and by leading me away from him, God was answering my prayers.

Something I still pray for is peace. I shared in chapter 8 that ever since James ghosted me, I've prayed every day that God will replace my sadness, anger, bitterness, and frustration with His peace. Even though I don't have complete peace, God has softened my heart to forgive James.

Around the same time I began praying for God's peace, I started memorizing Psalm 34. As I said in chapter 8, this chapter of Scripture really resonated with me as I grieved the end of the relationship. Over time, it stuck in my mind.

Another good thing I've seen God do through my experience with James is spur me to write. Honestly, I don't feel inspired in my writing very often—but I've written thousands of words about my experience with James. As God has comforted me with His Word and His presence, He's provided the words for me to share my relationship struggles and the lessons He's taught me through them.

If I hadn't met James or dated him or been hurt by him, I wouldn't have been able to write a significant portion of this book. Similarly, I wouldn't have been nearly as eager to get this book out into the world. My original plan was to get it published by a traditional publisher. Deep down, I knew I might need to self-publish it if I actually wanted people to have the opportunity to read it, but I was extremely attached to my original plan. I began praying daily for God to help me care more about encouraging single girls through this book than getting a traditional publisher. I needed Him to help me loosen my grip on *my* plan and be open to *His* plan. God worked in my heart and my circumstances for many months. Ultimately, all my attempts to get a book deal from a traditional publisher failed—but it wasn't until after my experience with James that I genuinely felt willing to self-publish this book. That experience fueled my desire to reach single girls and offer them encouragement about dating.

In addition, if I hadn't gone out with James, I wouldn't have been able to write an article about first dates for a Christian ministry. I actually wrote it while James and I were dating—before I knew our relationship was going to end. But the day after our third date, I submitted the article for publication. Three days later, the ministry director responded, expressing a desire to publish it. I knew the opportunity was from God because I just happened to get her email within hours of my first post-James cry. I'd sent countless articles to the ministry for publication over the years, but only two had been published—and this one would be the third.

Single Girl, because of James, I can connect with you on a deeper level. Pre-James, I wouldn't have been able to truly empathize with your relationship struggles, but now I can. And as a fellow single girl who understands what you're going through, I want you to keep something in mind: Even if you can't make sense of a relationship because it turned out differently than you planned, you can know it happened for a reason—and you can know God's plan for you is better. (In fact, it's *perfect*.)

God doesn't expect you to predict the outcome of a relationship. After all, you're human—you can't see the future. He simply wants you to commit your plans to Him and make decisions that honor Him. If you seek His will about dating a particular guy, He'll guide you to the right choice through Scripture, prayer, and people—and if you have peace about dating him because you've sought and heeded godly wisdom, you can trust that no matter how the relationship goes, it isn't wasted.

Erica's Story

I didn't start dating my now-husband, Justin, until over a decade after I met him. We actually met at a Christian boarding school when we were teenagers. He remembers the first time he saw me, and he immediately knew he wanted to get to know me. But I wasn't interested in dating him, so we became friends but nothing more.

After Justin and I graduated from high school, we didn't really stay in touch. I went away to college and started dating a guy I *thought* would become my husband. Our relationship felt serious, but it didn't last.

I moved out of state for a teaching job when I finished college. Right before I moved, Justin stopped by my family's house. As we talked, I wondered if perhaps I did like him—but I *highly* doubted he still had a crush on me. (He did, but I didn't know that yet!) Since I was going to move soon, I dismissed the idea of us becoming anything more than friends.

Over the next four years, Justin and I hardly saw each other. I had several romantic relationships, but most of them weren't healthy. I felt discouraged because guys didn't seem genuinely interested in me—at least not in *marrying* me.

In addition to that, I found out that the school I worked for wasn't going to offer me a contract to teach the next year. Weary and disappointed, I went home for spring break. To my surprise, Justin came over during my visit. He didn't say much to me, so I again dismissed the idea of us dating.

But that wasn't the end of our story. A few weeks after spring break, Justin texted me. In fact, we started texting and talking on the phone quite often. We got to see each other at an event in my home state and spent some time together. When I returned to my teaching job to finish the school year, we parted ways without establishing anything relationally. However, I didn't want to waste my time developing a serious relationship with him if he wasn't interested, so during our next phone call, I asked, "Justin, are we more than friends?"

My directness surprised him. Although he hoped our friendship would develop into something more, he assumed I wasn't ready for that yet. However, after that phone conversation, he drove eight hours to visit me, which made me realize he was serious. We got married a year later.

We've been married for almost five years and now have a daughter. Being married and having children are two deep desires I had as a young woman, and I'm thankful God fulfilled both of them. But He was working behind the scenes long before Justin and I got married.

I didn't find out about this until after high school, but when I dated Justin's roommate during high school and he told Justin about our relationship, Justin literally cried and begged God, "Please don't let Erica marry anyone else!" Obviously, my relationship with Justin's roommate didn't work out—and none of my other relationships did either. But God was answering Justin's prayer (and the prayers of many other people) through those broken relationships. In hindsight, I can see that as I walked through seasons filled with questions and heartache, God was guiding, preparing, and protecting me (and Justin).

~Erica, Former Single Girl~

Chapter 10

My Waiting ~~Is~~ Isn't Wasted

Dear Single Girl,

Even though I barely had a relationship with James, the transition from waiting to dating to waiting again was very difficult. The familiar feelings of emptiness and loneliness that had exited my life for about a month returned with a vengeance. A feeling that accompanied them was the feeling that I was back in the wilderness. When I was dating James, it felt like *something* was happening—but since then, it's felt like *nothing* is happening.

I've literally gone on one date since my relationship with James ended. At the walk-and-talk event that I mentioned in chapters 7 and 8, multiple guys I spoke with piqued my curiosity, including a guy named Aaron. When the event ended, I checked off the boxes next to their names on a notecard, indicating I was interested in connecting with them. Then I handed the notecard to Kendra, and I later received an email from her with my matches—the guys I'd indicated interest in connecting with who had indicated interest in connecting with me.

Of my three matches, Aaron was the only guy brave enough to ask me out. Though I said yes, I wondered if I only wanted to go out with him because I was on the rebound. After all, James was clearly moving on. I was worried about getting left behind.

However, Aaron and I didn't vibe on our date. In fact, I headed home from the restaurant after only an hour. (Spoiler alert: We didn't go out a second time.) I was officially single again, and I hated it. I wanted to date—and ultimately move toward marriage—not feel stuck in singleness.

Single Girl, perhaps you've been led to believe your waiting is wasted because people in your life have said or implied things like, "Marriage provides so many great opportunities for growth" or even "Singleness breeds selfishness." Unfortunately, the idea that marriage is superior to singleness is conveyed by many people, including those who didn't have to wait very long to find love. Though you probably *can't* change their views on your relationship status, you *can* focus on what Scripture says—or rather, what it *doesn't* say—about your relationship status. It *never* says marriage is superior to singleness. In fact, it clearly communicates that God values marriage *and* singleness and can use *both* seasons to sanctify you.

I realize it might feel like nothing is happening in this season. After all, no one is dating you, texting you, or even trying to get to know you. But the Lord is doing an important thing in your life while you wait to find love: He's preparing you. He's working right here, right now. For that very reason, your waiting isn't wasted.

Love, Grace

During my childhood, I played several seasons of soccer. By far, the best part of playing soccer was being on the field. It meant I could truly contribute to my team's success. Plus, it meant receiving attention and applause.

But the players on the sidelines were generally overlooked. As they sat and watched the game, they waited for a chance to participate. They wondered when the coach would call their names so they could run onto the field to play alongside everyone else.

I've been on the sidelines of relationships for most of my life. I've wished my friends congratulations when I've received their save-the-dates and wedding invitations. I've attended their bridal showers and bachelorette parties with smiles, laughter, and gifts. I've clapped and cheered during their wedding ceremonies and receptions. I've listened to them talk about their honeymoon getaways and anniversary trips. And I've waited for my turn to come.

For a few minutes—literally a few weeks—I got to be on the field. My name was called for the very first time. A tall, dark, and handsome guy named James wanted to go out with me. At last, I had the chance to sprint down the field, kick the ball into the goal, and hear the crowd clap and cheer for me.

But before I could score a single point, I heard my name being called again.

"Grace! Get off the field! Holly is going to switch with you!"

As Holly ran onto the field to take my place, I resumed my position on the sidelines. Fighting the urge to cry—and despair—I watched, wondered, and waited. Again.

To be honest, I didn't expect to spend so much of my life on the sidelines of relationships. After all, when I was growing up, there was far more emphasis on dating than waiting. The Christian books I read, the youth group lessons I heard, and the Bible studies I attended prepared me to date but not to wait. I was encouraged to commit to sexual purity and establish boundaries in relationships, but I don't recall being encouraged to trust that God's plan for me was good even when I was date-less.

I remember going to camp the summer before my freshman year of high school and listening to a pastor compare abstinence to a donut shop during one of his messages. He said something like, "Don't go in the donut shop if you're not actually going to buy a donut." Basically, he meant, "Don't do anything that could *lead* to sex if you're not ready to actually *have* sex."

I thought the metaphor was clever. But since I wasn't allowed to date for several more years, it wasn't particularly relevant at the time. Plus, I already knew I wasn't supposed to have sex before I got married.

I had another interesting experience during camp, but it involved a dress code violation, not a donut shop sermon. Before arriving at camp, I learned about the dress code and packed my duffel bag accordingly. But I didn't realize how strict it was until the last night of camp—aka banquet night. The only real difference between banquet night and every other night at camp was that everyone dressed up. (Oh, and some campers attended as couples. How romantic, right?) In my mind, the banquet was practically a royal ball at the castle.

I wore a lovely turquoise dress to the banquet. But while I was sitting in the dining hall, a camp counselor approached me and told me to go to my cabin to change. Apparently, my lovely turquoise dress violated the dress code. My straps—which literally weren't even straps because they were four inches wide—were a potential stumbling block to my fellow campers. (Pardon my sarcasm.) Speechless, I hurried back to my cabin to find something else to wear. I ended up putting on a cardigan to cover my scandalous straps. Feeling a mixture of anger and embarrassment, I returned to the dining hall for the royal ball (ahem, *banquet*).

Obviously, this story would be incomplete without a camp crush, so I'll go ahead and introduce Derrick, the cute camp lifeguard. During my weeklong stay at camp, we had one interaction, which occurred while I was searching for Anna's retainers. She went to camp with me—which I greatly appreciated because I wouldn't have survived the week without her—but she lost her retainers partway through the week and wanted me to help her find them. (What good are younger sisters if they won't help their older sisters retrieve their lost retainers?)

As Anna and I were looking through bags of trash outside the dining hall, Derrick stopped by to see what we were doing. But instead of offering to help us find the retainers, he made a joke—which I don't remember, unfortunately—and proceeded to walk away. Another unfortunate part of this story is that we couldn't find the retainers.

When I went home from camp, I took several lessons with me: Enter the donut shop only when appropriate, wear dresses with very thick straps, and avoid crushing on immature camp lifeguards no matter how cute they are. (More broadly, my takeaways were: Save sex for marriage, dress modestly, and have high standards.) Were those good lessons for me to learn? Definitely. But were they the *only* good lessons for me to learn? Definitely *not*. I really wish someone at camp—or *several* people at camp—had talked about relying on God to provide my future husband, dealing with the pain of unrequited love, and holding on to hope during the wait—because even though I didn't know it at the time, I'd really need encouragement in those areas.

But my camp experiences weren't *completely* negative because they—along with several similar experiences—ultimately inspired me to write this book. Years after the donut shop sermon, the dress code violation, and the cliché camp crush, I made the realization that in the Church, there's far more emphasis on dating than waiting. While marriage is put on a pedestal, singleness is disregarded or even looked down on. Even though waiting for the Lord is frequently commanded in Scripture, it's rarely discussed in the Church (especially among young people).

I genuinely empathize with the single girl who feels like a soccer player on the sidelines—the one who's waiting for God to lead the right guy to her but being treated like she's not a contributing member of the team until that time comes. She can't help but feel stagnant and insignificant in her current season of life. After all, she's told that her sole purpose for right now is to clap and cheer for her teammates who are on the field.

Some people assume she's still single because she's too busy chasing a career to have a family or because she's being too picky or because she's not doing enough to meet guys. Few realize she's still single because she's trusting God to provide her future husband in His time and in His way. Similarly, few realize she deeply desires to meet her future husband and needs the same level of support that dating, engaged, and married people receive while she waits for God to lead him into her life.

Single Girl, do you sometimes feel like a soccer player on the sidelines? Since you've stayed with me up to this point in the book, I assume the answer is yes. I wish I could silence the false narratives that have led you to feel that way, but since I can't, I want to encourage you with this truth that I've had to tell myself on countless occasions: No matter how you feel or how people treat you, you're not on the sidelines. In fact, *no* followers of Jesus are on the sidelines except the ones who choose to sit there. The decision to approach this season with intentionality—or passivity—is yours.

//

> "All the commandments that I am commanding you today you shall be careful to do, that you may live and multiply, and go in and possess the land which the LORD swore to give to your forefathers. You shall remember all the way which the LORD your God has led you in the wilderness these forty years, that He might humble you, testing you, to know what was in your heart, whether you would keep His commandments or not. He humbled you and let you be hungry, and fed you with manna which you did not know, nor did your fathers know, that He might make you understand that man does not live by bread alone, but man lives by everything that proceeds out of the mouth of the LORD. Your clothing did not wear out on you, nor did your foot swell these forty years. Thus you are to know in your heart that the LORD your God was disciplining you just as a man disciplines his son. Therefore, you shall keep the commandments of the LORD your God, to walk in His ways and to fear Him. For the LORD your God is bringing you into a good land, a land of brooks of water, of fountains and springs, flowing forth in valleys and hills; a land of wheat and barley, of vines and fig trees and pomegranates, a land of olive oil and honey; a land where you will eat food without scarcity, in which you will not lack anything; a land whose stones are iron, and out of whose hills you can dig copper. When you have eaten and are satisfied, you shall bless the

> LORD your God for the good land which He has given you." (Deut. 8:1-10 NASB)

I'm sure the Israelites were extremely eager to finish the journey through the wilderness and enter the Promised Land. But as they longed for what was ahead—a land where water flowed through hills and valleys, iron and copper emerged from the earth, and food never became scarce—God sustained them where they were. I believe that both their season in the wilderness and their season in the Promised Land were important.

Writing about Deuteronomy 8:14-16 (a passage from the same chapter as the passage I shared), Kelly Needham explained how God was at work in the Israelites' lives: "He was leading them, feeding them, and humbling them so that they would recognize that he was their provider. God was trying to cultivate their dependency on him, not on people. He is often up to the same things in us: leading us, and sustaining us, and helping us see it's God we really need."[1]

I believe that in our season of singleness, the Lord humbles us, tests us, disciplines us, and lets us be hungry—for attention, affection, love, intimacy, and sex—because in the "letting," He teaches us invaluable lessons. I definitely get discouraged about my lack of a romantic relationship. However, God has helped me see singleness differently as He's whispered, "Grace, I'm letting you be hungry—in this area of your life, for this season of your life—because I love you."

Yes, marriage is a wonderful blessing from the Lord that we can eagerly anticipate (and should certainly thank Him for when He provides it). But before we enter that season, we're called to wait. We're called to have patience, dependence, and hope, knowing He sustains us—and blesses us—even in the seasons that feel dry and deserted like the wilderness.

The writer of Hebrews pointed out one specific blessing that comes from God's discipline: "For [our earthly fathers] disciplined us for a short time as it seemed best to them, but he disciplines us for our good, that we may share his holiness. For the moment all discipline seems painful rather than pleasant, but later it yields the peaceful fruit of righteousness to those who have been trained by it" (Heb. 12:10-11 ESV).

God uses difficult situations to test our faith in Him and prove its genuineness (1 Pet. 1:6-7). Singleness can be a very painful trial, but He promises that if we allow Him to shape us through it, He will. It *does* have a purpose.

Another passage from Scripture that God has used to show me the significance of singleness is this one: "An excellent wife, who can find? For her worth is far above jewels. The heart of her husband trusts in her, and he will have no lack of gain. She does him good and not evil all the days of her life" (Prov. 31:10-12 NASB).

The woman in Proverbs 31 is typically mentioned when Christians teach wives and mothers about loving God, their husbands, and their children. But several months ago, the Lord helped me see this passage in a new way. King Lemuel, who wrote Proverbs 31, described the woman as excellent, rare, valuable, and trustworthy. I found verse 12 particularly interesting because it says she does her husband good *all* the days of her life, not just the days of her life as a *married* woman. Maybe I'm reading too much into that verse, but I doubt she suddenly became an amazing woman when she got married. In fact, it's possible that her efforts to honor her husband began long before she even met him. As God opened my eyes to this possibility, He revealed the relevance of King Lemuel's words in my own life.

Will my future husband view me as an excellent wife whose worth is far above jewels? I asked myself. *Will his heart trust in me? Am I doing him good and not evil all the days of my life—including in this season while I'm waiting for him?*

I know that my main goal in life shouldn't be to please people—including the man I'll marry one day. But I also know that the decisions I make now that honor (or dishonor) God can honor (or dishonor) my future husband too. Even the choices that seem small and insignificant can profoundly affect my marriage—for better or worse.

It's easy to feel like God isn't doing anything while I'm waiting. However, that's simply a feeling—it's not reality. Not only is He sustaining me during this season, but He's also preparing me for the next season.

Single Girl, I realize that preparing for marriage might seem less important than actually being married. But entering marriage prepared is an incredible gift you can give your future husband one day. You can become an excellent wife before you even meet him—and waiting provides an opportunity for that to happen.

As you consider how to prepare for marriage, you might want to ask yourself the following questions:

1. Am I reading the Bible, praying, and attending/serving at church regularly?
2. Am I seeking to build God's kingdom by sharing the gospel with non-Christians and by helping other Christians grow in their faith?

3. Am I investing in the people and the relationships God has given me?
4. Am I generating enough income to meet all my needs, set aside money for emergency situations, and give to individuals and organizations as God leads me?
5. Am I walking in freedom from addictions (such as addictions to alcohol, pornography, and social media)?
6. Am I wearing clothes that cover the parts of my body I want to reserve for my future husband?
7. Am I treating guys (including guys I date) with care and consideration—not only for them but also for their future wives and my future husband?
8. Am I reading, listening to, and watching content (including content on social media and in books, songs, shows, and movies) that I wouldn't mind my future husband reading, listening to, and watching?

Honestly, I only feel confident answering yes to a few of those questions. For a time, I actually kept a framed note on my desk with the question "Would I want my future husband to look at this?" as a reminder to be careful about the content I view. I've viewed plenty of content—especially online content—that I wouldn't want my future husband to view. I'm thankful that God offers forgiveness and that His plan prevails even when I sin, but I don't want to enter marriage with lots of issues I need to work through—especially because I can work through them *right now*. You can too. Approaching the wait with intentionality is key to finding purpose in it and growing through it.

Just like every other challenging season of life, singleness is an opportunity. It's an opportunity to turn from God or run to Him. It's an opportunity to cling to your plans or open your hands. It's an opportunity to give in to fear or rest in His love. He's fully capable of changing your relationship status, but your faith in Him can't grow unless you follow Him in seasons of ease *and* in seasons of hardship. He promises to love you through both.

Until the time comes for you to get married, don't allow false narratives to lead you into despair. Instead, be strong, let your heart take courage, and wait for the Lord. I'm waiting right here with you, Single Girl.

//

Jennifer's Story

I tell my three daughters that being single was the most difficult thing I've ever done—probably because it required so much faith. Other difficult things I've done haven't made me feel so helpless. Singleness demanded that I trust God completely to work in my situation. I didn't know what was going to happen. I didn't know when—or even *if*—singleness would come to an end. And I didn't have a specific biblical promise to hold on to.

I wish I'd trusted God more. I wish I'd had more reliance on His timeline. I wish I'd rested in the knowledge that He had a good plan for *all* of my life.

Singleness did have a purpose. It wasn't a waste of time. I could've looked at it as simply a season of my life. But all I could do was wonder when singleness would end and hope it would end soon.

But in His mercy, the Lord worked all things together for my good (Rom. 8:28). After waiting for many years, I finally met my husband. Not long before that, my brother gave me the best piece of advice I ever received as a single woman. He told me to pray I'd be the gift God would give to a man, as Solomon wrote in this proverb: "He who finds a wife finds a good thing and obtains favor from the LORD" (Prov. 18:22 NASB).

~Jennifer, Former Single Girl (and My Mom)~

Notes

Chapter 3: Friendship ~~Is~~ Isn't Equivalent to Marriage

1. Taken from Friend-ish: Reclaiming Real Friendship in a Culture of Confusion by Kelly Needham Copyright © 2019 by Kelly Needham. Used by permission of HarperCollins Christian Publishing. www.harpercollinschristian.com
2. Taken from Friend-ish: Reclaiming Real Friendship in a Culture of Confusion by Kelly Needham Copyright © 2019 by Kelly Needham. Used by permission of HarperCollins Christian Publishing. www.harpercollinschristian.com

Chapter 10: My Waiting ~~Is~~ Isn't Wasted

1. Taken from Friend-ish: Reclaiming Real Friendship in a Culture of Confusion by Kelly Needham Copyright © 2019 by Kelly Needham. Used by permission of HarperCollins Christian Publishing. www.harpercollinschristian.com

Acknowledgements

God: Though I don't know all the details of Your plan for my life, I know it's a perfect plan—and I trust it because I trust You. I can have peace about the past, purpose in the present, and hope for the future. Thank You for Your faithfulness in my season of singleness (and in *every* season of my life).

Dad and Mom: Your story inspires me. I'm so thankful you were willing to wait for each other. Thank you for encouraging me to wait for the man God ordained for me to marry, praying for him since I was born, and giving me an incredible example to follow.

Anna and Jenna: You're so much more than sisters; you're my best friends. You always have been—and always will be—my favorite companions. I'm grateful for the time we've gotten to spend together in this post-college, pre-marriage season of life.

Friends and collaborators: Thank you to the endorsers who offered kind feedback about this book. Thank you to the single girls and former single girls who provided their perspectives on singleness. And thank you to everyone who's encouraged, supported, and prayed for me—not only as I've shared my dating and waiting experiences in these pages but also as I've lived them.

About the Author

Grace McCready is a writer and speaker who is passionate about encouraging young women through personal stories and scriptural truths. She is the author of *The Ring by Spring Ruse* and *Real Recovery*, and she blogs at *Tizzie's Tidbits of Truth*. She is also a full-time writer/editor for a Christian ministry.

www.ingramcontent.com/pod-product-compliance
Lightning Source LLC
LaVergne TN
LVHW020636100826
845148LV00012B/2202

9798218896829